Kauai Island, the Garden Isle

Travel and Tourism

Author
Kenneth Butler

Copyright Notice

Copyright © 2017 Global Print Digital
All Rights Reserved

Digital Management Copyright Notice. This Title is not in public domain, it is copyrighted to the original author, and being published by **Global Print Digital**. No other means of reproducing this title is accepted, and none of its content is editable, neither right to commercialize it is accepted, except with the consent of the author or authorized distributor. You must purchase this Title from a vendor who's right is given to sell it, other sources of purchase are not accepted, and accountable for an action against. We are happy that you understood, and being guided by these terms as you proceed. Thank you

First Printing: 2017.

ISBN: 978-1-912483-05-1

Publisher: Global Print Digital.
Arlington Row, Bibury, Cirencester GL7 5ND
Gloucester
United Kingdom.
Website: www.homeworkoffer.com

Table of Content

Touristic Introduction 1
History 4
   Kauai's history at a glance 4
   In the beginning 5
   Cook's arrival 7
   Kauai and the Kingdom of Hawaii 8
   Spread of Christianity 8
   Economic evolution 9
   Kauai in present times 11
The People and Culture 13
   The Cultural Scene in Kauai 13
   The People of Kauai 20
      Kauai Festivals & Events 26
Tourism 29
   Tourist Attractions and Festivals in Kauai 37
   Activities and Attractions 44
      Biking 44
      Boat Tours 45
      Health & Rejuvenation 46
      Hiking 46
      Horseback Tours 47
      Luau 48
      Surfing & Stand Up Paddling 49
      Ziplining on Kauai 50
      Whale Watching on Kauai 51
      Snorkeling and Scuba on Kauai 52
      Kauai Gardens & Parks 53
      Kayaking on Kauai 54
      Hula on Kauai 55
      Whale Watching on Kauai 56
      Kauai's Scenic Byways 57
      Kauai Restaurants & Food on the Coconut Coast 58
   Historic Places of Kauai 59
      Waimea Canyon 61
      Daniel K. Inouye Kilauea Point Lighthouse 62
      Waimea Town 63
      Hanapepe Town 64
      Old Koloa Town 65

Koloa Heritage Trail, Kauai 66
　　Hanalei Town 69
　　Waioli Huuia Church and Mission House 70
　　Grove Farm Homestead Museum 72
　　Lihue, Kauai 73
　　Kauai Museum 74
　　Alekoko Fishpond 75
　　Napali Coast 76
Accommodations in Kauai 77
　　Aston Islander on the Beach 85
　　Aston at Poipu Kai Formerly Resort Quest 87
　　Aston Waimea Plantation Cottages 90
　　Castle Kaha Lani, A Condominium Resort 93
　　Castle Kiahuna Plantation & Beach Bungalows 95
　　Castle Lae Nani, A Condominium Resort 98
　　Castle Kiahuna Plantation & Beach Bungalows 101
　　Castle Lae Nani, A Condominium Resort 104
　　Castle Lanikai, A Condominium Resort 106
　　Castle Makahuena, A Condominium Resort At Poipu 109
　　Wyndham Bali Hai Villas 112
　　Whalers Cove Oceanfront Condominiums 115
　　Westin Princeville Ocean Resort Villas 117
　　The Point At Poipu 120
　　Pono Kai/Bluegreen Resort 123
East Kauai *125*
　　How to Get to East Kauai 131
　　What to Do in East Kauai 134
　　Where to Stay in East Kauai 141
　　Fixed Budget 146
North Kauai *152*
　　How to Get to North Kauai 158
　　What to Do in North Kauai 161
　　Where to Stay in North Kauai 166
　　Fixed Budget 173
West Kauai *179*
　　How to Get to West Kauai 185
　　What to Do in West Kauai 187
　　Where to Stay in West Kauai 194
　　Fixed Budget 199

Touristic Introduction

On any list of the world's most spectacular islands, Kauai ranks right up there with Bora Bora, Huahine, and Rarotonga. All the elements are here: moody rainforests, majestic cliffs, jagged peaks, emerald valleys, palm trees swaying in the breeze, daily rainbows, and some of the most spectacular golden beaches you'll find anywhere. Soft tropical air, sunrise bird song, essences of ginger and plumeria, golden sunsets, sparkling waterfalls -- you don't just go to Kauai, you absorb it with every sense. This is the place for people who need to relax and heal jangled nerves, as well as those looking for hiking, swimming, golfing, and other adventures.

Beaches: On an island with some of the world's best beaches, you'll have no trouble finding the perfect one for you. On the North Shore, gentle waves roll across the golden sands of half-moon Hanalei Bay, where sheer volcanic ridges laced by waterfalls rise to 4,000 feet in the background, making it perfect for swimming, surfing, fishing, canoe paddling, and kayaking. On the south shore, big, wide Poipu Beach features a lava-rock jetty, protecting a sandy-bottomed pool that's perfect for children on one side and an open bay attracting swimmers, snorkelers, and surfers on the other.

Things to Do: Soar over the dramatic Na Pali Coast. The only way to see the spectacular, surreal beauty of Kauai is via a helicopter: dipping low over razor-thin cliffs, fluttering past sparkling waterfalls, and swooping down into the canyons and valleys of the fabled Waimea Canyon. The only problem is that there's too much beauty to absorb, and it all goes by in a rush. And plunge beneath the waves -- you haven't really seen Kauai until you have seen the magical world underwater.

Eating & Drinking: A trip to Kauai is not complete without indulging in Hawaii's culinary specialty, the luau. The oceanfront Mediterranean Gourmet is one of the island's best commercial luau, where you are treated to a traditional feast of kalua pig cooked in an imu (an underground pit lined with hot rocks to cook the pig), poi (a starch made from taro, which has the consistency of library paste with little or no taste), best combined with salty lomi salmon (chopped onions, tomatoes, and salmon), savory sweet potatoes, a crunchy fern shoot salad, and for dessert, haupia (coconut pudding).

Nature: Hike the spectacular beauty of the Na Pali Coast or the drama of the Waimea Canyon. Explore the beauty of rushing waterfalls thundering downward into sparkling freshwater pools, like the accessible 40-foot Opaekaa Falls. Or smell the sweet scent of flowers at Kauai's spectacular range of tropical flora in gardens like Na Aina Kai Botanical Gardens on the North Shore, or Allerton Garden in Poipu and Limahuli outside of Hanalei.

History

Being the oldest populated main island in Hawaii, you can be sure that Kauai has a lot of history. It has gone through a lot through the ages, from its ancient roots and first settlers, to the arrival of the Westerners, and to its current form as part of a state under the US. As such, Kauai has been at the forefront of the changes of the times, easily leaving a historic footprint on the island. Aside from the natural beauty of its vegetation and surroundings, Kawai is also ripe with all of the influence of man since his first arrival on the island's shores.

Kauai's history at a glance

200 to 600 AD -- Early Marquesans arrived at the island

1778 -- James Cook arrived at the shores of Kauai

1810 -- The Kingdom of Hawaii was established under the rule of Kamehameha the Great, which included the island of Kauai

1820 -- The first mission house in Wiamea was built

Early 19th century -- Economic evolution surged due to the sugar and pineapple industries

1893 -- The Hawaii of Kingdom was overthrown

1920s -- The tourism industry in Kauai was born

1959 -- Hawaii, along with Kauai, became the 50th state of the United States of America

In the beginning

According to archeological findings, Kauai was inhabited as early as 200 to 600 AD. It was theorized that these settlers reached Kauai on double-hulled sea vessels from Marquesas Islands, which is about 2,000 miles away. These early settlers also brought with them taro, sweet potato, sugar cane, and other plants from their land of origin.

It's believed that these first settlers were the only humans who have seen the pristine state of Kauai. Since then, it is said that about 1,000 of the 1,300 species of plants and animals in Kauai suffered extinction from the arrival of the early Polynesians to the arrival of the European settlers.

It is also theorized that the original settlers were the short Marquesans, which were then chased away by the taller and stronger Tahitians who came later. A lot of folklore was made about the

Marquesans, or the Menehune, and in modern times, they are believed to be responsible for bad luck.

What is certain is that the early settlers of Kauai were proficient farmers and fishermen. These people knew how to use and make tools out of bone and stone, and knew where the good fishing and octopus spots were. They were also able to establish farming and irrigation techniques that ensured the survival of their crops. In a way, the early settlers were innovative in finding means for their survival.

Centuries later, the Tahitians came and, as mentioned, the Marquesans were overrun. The next wave of Polynesian immigrants formed the race of Hawaiians that is known today.

The early settlers have a civilized form of society, with evidence of religion and laws. Such evidence include the tradition that states Wailua as a sacred birthing ground. Members of the royalty go to Wailua to give birth to their young, believing in the special significance, blessing, and nobility that the area grants to their offspring. This tradition is so well-set that according to a song, a nobility not born in Wailua is considered a commoner, and a commoner born in the area can be considered a nobility. Another proof of the ancient Hawaiian's religious system and laws is the existence of heaius or temples that were built by these early people for worshipping their gods. These temples can still be found in the Wailua River.

Cook's arrival

It was still centuries later before Kauai and Hawaii will become known to the whole of the Western world. It was in Kauai in 1778, when James Cook arrived in Waimea Bay with his ships the HMS Discovery and Resolution, that Hawaii would be changed forever. Cook first named Hawaii as the Sandwich Islands as a tribute to his benefactor, the 4th Earl of Sandwich. However, there are accounts that it was not Cook who first discovered Kauai and Hawaii but Gaetan, a Spanish navigator. Be that as it may, it does not change the large significance of Cook's arrival and discovery of Kauai. It was due to Cook's arrival that Hawaii opened up to the ideas, culture, and influence of the Western world, leading to events that forever changed the history of Hawaii, its culture, and its people.

One of the negative impacts of the arrival of the European settlers was the diseases that they brought with them. Since the bodies of the Hawaiians did not have immunity to these diseases, it resulted to an endemic and the native population was drastically reduced by the thousands.

Kauai and the Kingdom of Hawaii

Kamehameha I has all of Hawaii subjugated except for Kauai. The then ruler of Kauai, Kaumuali'i, resisted Kamehameha's assaults, and was saved from Kamehameha's first conquest because of a storm that led to the sinking of Kamehameha's armada. A persistent leader, Kamehameha once again launched an attack on the island of Kauai. It seemed that the gods may have favored Kaumuali'i because the second attack failed because of the spread of cholera. However, using his skills as a wise leader, Kaumuali'i decided to give up his kingdom in a peaceful manner to Kamehameha during a third attack. Because of this seemingly wise decision, Kaumuali'i retained his rank and title in exchange for the surrender. Thus, the first united Kingdom of Hawaii under the rule of Kamehameha I was born.

Spread of Christianity

The religious belief systems of the Hawaiians went through a drastic change when the first Christian missionaries reached the shores of Kauai. The earliest missionaries who arrived in Kauai were from New England. The fist mission house was constructed in Waimea in 1820. Biblical laws were in place, and the old Tahitian kapu system was set away. One can say that there was a slow destruction of the native culture in Hawaii, as what usually happens in other colonized nations.

As the Christian religion gained much influence on the ruling class, notably Ka'ahumanu, the widow of Kamehameha I, changes were also made to the political system of Hawaii. From an absolute monarchy, the government was transformed into a constitutional monarchy, where the laws and tenets were based or derived from Biblical laws and beliefs. During this time, Western settlers have also started to have influence due to their economic stakes in Hawaii.

One good result of missionary influence in Hawaii is the translation and recording of the native Hawaiian language in written form. As missionaries sought to translate the Bible into the vernacular, the once purely oral language of Hawaii has been set in writing, ensuring its preservation.

Economic evolution

The next phase in the Kauai's history is the evolution of its economy. Driven by the enterprising spirit of the Westerners, Kauai was transformed into one of the chief sugar producers during the early part of the 19th century. Kauai's Koloa town was witness to the establishment of a historic sugar mill that lead to an economic surge. The success of this first-ever mill prompted others to join the sugar industry. This success lasted for a century, and it brought affluence to the sugar plantation owners and Hawaii itself.

One of the effects of the sugar boom in Hawaii is the influx of immigrants from different nations. As the native population is not sufficient to provide the needed workforce to keep the plantations going, immigrant laborers came from different regions to meet the demand. Most of the immigrants came from Japan, China, Puerto Rico, Philippines, and Portugal. This arrival of different immigrants contributed to the multi-cultural flavor of Kauai and Hawaii as a whole.

The next economic opportunity for Kauai is the pineapple industry. The prominent company in Kauai that was involved in pineapple production was the Kauai Fruit and Land Co. which held operations in Lawa'i. The company lasted from the early 1900s to the early 1960s. Another company, Hawaiian Canneries Co. Ltd., also did not last long as it also closed in the early 1960s.

After the rise and fall of the sugar and pineapple industry in Hawaii, the next boom in Kauai economy is tourism. As the numbers of visitors grew, so did the establishment of hotels and resorts in the island. This created thousands of jobs and new opportunities for large and small businesses alike. Currently, tourism accounts for one-third of the income of Kauai. Previous sugar plantations have now been transformed to resorts and ranches. There are also plans to use sugar cane as means to produce ethanol.

It is because of these economic interests that certain groups of foreigners conducted an overthrow of the Kingdom of Hawaii in 1893. As the constitution was being amended at the time and those amendments were against the interests of foreigners in Hawaii, the revolution took place and Hawaii was eventually annexed to the US as a territory in the 1900s, and became an official state in 1959.

Kauai in present times

Kauai has gone a long way from its origins. As for its tourism, the Kauai Island is now noted for its rich vegetation, collection of historical landmarks, and its nature and wildlife. Some of the places to see in Kauai are Kauai Museum, Kamokila Hawaiian Village, Kilauea Lighthouse, Koke'e Natural History Museum, and the Heiau of Wailua. These places should give visitors a good feel of the history of Kauai and how it evolved to its present state.

If one wants to know Hawaiian history, then one should definitely take Kauai into consideration. Being one of the oldest islands and rich with Hawaiian history and culture, Kauai has played a large role in the forming of the identity of Hawaii today. Aside from welcoming the first

Polynesian settlers, Europeans, and missionaries, Kauai also was the first to welcome and experience the dynamic changes that these events brought. Kauai has within its borders all things essentially Hawaii, from the native culture, to the diverse and mixed multi-national culture that is present in Hawaii today. So if you want a good view of Hawaii, then you should also get a good look at Kauai

The People and Culture
The Cultural Scene in Kauai

The cultural attractions of Kauai is among the most unique of the Hawaiian islands, despite the fact that most of the Hawaiians islands already have a unique culture all on their own. The Garden Isle is a land with a rich and varied culture, as seen in its local theater performers, songs, dance, music, language, food, and native arts. Its unique culture also pervades the whole island with the ready and happy smiles of its locals who were born with and live in the spirit of aloha.

The spirit of aloha

A large part of the culture in Kauai is the spirit of aloha. This is the spirit that makes the Kauai natives one of the happiest and friendliest people among the inhabitants of the Hawaiian islands. While there is no doubt that living in paradise is one way to keep dissatisfied grumblings at bay, locals are happy and friendly because they have been raised in the spirit of aloha, the spirit that seeks to find good in everyone, whether one is a friend or a stranger.

The Hawaiian luau

A visit to any of the Hawaiian islands will not be complete without participating in a Hawaiian luau, which is a traditional Hawaiian feast that is celebrated as soon as the sun starts to go down. This is where tourists get to experience a rich facet of Kauai culture, from the food to the dancing to the entertainment, all in one night. The luau is where most tourists will get to see the aloha spirit in action. The center of any Kauai luau is the food. Every traditional luau has the kalua pork or roasted pig, which is prepared early in the morning of the luau. The pig is cooked on red hot coals on top of a bed of banana leaves. The pig is then covered in sand to cook, made soft by the steam created by the banana coverings and the fiery hot coals. Cooking the pig takes about 6 to 8 hours.

This is not the only gustatory offering in a traditional luau, however. Guests will also have the opportunity to sample other local dishes such as poi, chicken long rice, haupia, and many more. And of course, no luau will be complete without refreshments. Drinks with Hawaiian roots such as Mai Tais are also usually served during luaus. Luaus are outdoor affairs and are usually held at the beach, where everyone can enjoy the cool breeze that comes from the ocean as they listen to traditional Hawaiian music or watch a group of locals dance the hula. Fire dancing is also another popular entertainment option in most Hawaiian luaus.

Making of leis

The lei, just like the hula, is one of the most recognizable images of Hawaii and its islands. In the islands, leis are symbols for harmony, friendship, and the start of new things. Presentation of the lei was often done on special occasions such as when people would gather to celebrate events, tasks, and other joyous moments. Leis are garlands of flowers that are strung together and the ends tied together. Another version of the lei is the maile, which is a garland of vines and leaves known for their sweet-smelling scent. It is also an island tradition to drape leis on special visitors and those who have come for the first time on the island.

Making of kapa cloths

Kapa making is the process of making fabrics from kapa or bark. This process is a tradition of most Hawaiian women who have learned from their mothers and grandmothers the long and difficult task of fashioning cloth from the barks of specific types of plants. The bark is first treated with saltwater for several days to make it soft. They are then removed from the water, laid out on a flat surface and pounded flat with a round pounder, after which they are again soaked. As soon as the strips dry and the kapa is finished, it is decorated with hand paintings and coated with oil to protect it from the rain and dampness. Then it is stored with flowers and other scented items so that it can soak up the fragrance.

The hula dance

No visit to the island is complete without seeing a group of locals performing the hula. The hula dance is the traditional Hawaiian dance that probably originated from Polynesian settlers and is the subject of numerous legends told from generation to generation. It is said that Molokai was the first-ever island to witness the hula dance.

The hula dance is a series of graceful movements that are actually interpretations of the mele or the song or chanting that is sang along with the hula dance. Locals use the mele to tell of their island's history, culture, and ancient ceremonies as a way to orally pass down their traditions from one generation to the next.

The two major styles of the hula dance are the kahiko and the auana. The kahiko is the ancient hula, the traditional way of dancing before Westerners set foot on the island. The auana is the hula style that developed in the 19th and 20th century which evolved as a result of the island's exposure to Westerners and is performed along with the music of the ukulele, the double bass and the guitar. Other exotic dances from Tahiti, Samoa, New Zealand, and other Polynesian islands are also performed in most cultural gatherings, but none have the distinctive Hawaiian flair displayed by the hula. During the 1800s, visiting missionaries who saw the locals dance the hula thought that it was too suggestive and had it outlawed. Today, the hula is one of the most distinctive cultural attractions in the Hawaiian islands.

Theater

Art and theater buffs will find the rich cultural heritage in theater that the island has. Numerous theatrical productions are staged on the island every year to entertain locals and tourists alike. The Kauai International Theater is one of the major cultural draws of the island and is located in Wailua. The theater is the setting of varied and numerous theatrical acts, from local plays to international productions, done every year. Guests are often treated to a special performance when local native performers take their turn on the stage. The theater can get really crowded especially during tourist months, so it's best to book for seats in advance.

Another cultural hub that centers on theater is the Raddison Kauai Beach Resort which is the setting for Broadway productions such as A

Nite of Broadway. The younger, theater-loving crowd may also be found at the Kauai Community College Performing Arts Center, where theater students often hold their performances.

Festivals

The island has no shortage of art and music festivals, from the Annual Kauai Mokihana Festival which lasts for eight days, to the one-day May Day or Lei Day, where everyone in the island gets to wear a lei. The Annual Kauai Mokihana Festival is an eight-day festival that celebrates local art and artists, as well as local musicians. Local artists open their studios to the public and musicians test their mettle against each other with musical competitions. There are also workshops on healing, guitar playing, and arts and crafts. October is yet another month of festivals, among them the Aloha Week Festival which features the best in Hawaiian song, dance, music, food, and more.

Another festival is the Hawaii International Film Festival which showcases Pacific Rim films. The festival is held in November and draws tourists and local moviegoers.

In June, tourists will get to partake in the O-Bon season, a festival to celebrate the Japanese settlers in the island and their history. After a moment of dancing, the descendants of Japanese immigrants send out lighted lanterns inside paper boats out to sea. In July, the Koloa plantations become alive during the Koloa Plantation Days, a festival characterized by a lot of dancing and merry making. The celebration lasts for a week and ends with a festive parade.

History

The island also has a good collection of historical artifacts and historical sites. Among them is the Kukui Heiau on Alakukui Point. This historical structure is on the registry of Hawaii and National Historic Places. One can also make a stop at the Koloa history Center which houses a collection of photos of the island's past.

The Kauai Museum is another stop for those who want to know more about the island's history. Other places of interest include the Kokee Natural History Museum, historical towns such as Hanalei, Hanapepe, and Lihue, and the Waioli Mission House.

When looking for cultural attractions and sights to see in Kauai, you will never run out of options as this Hawaiian island boasts of plenty of monuments, museums, festivals, performances, and sacred grounds that tell the story of this island's rich Polynesian culture and history. To make the most out of your vacation in Kauai, make sure to include the abovementioned sights, performances, and cultural attractions in your itinerary.

The People of Kauai

The Garden Isle's pristine ruggedness, sparkling white beaches, and luxurious accommodations amidst lush tropical paradise are not the only things that make this Hawaiian island unique. Kauai's people are also an important part of its charm and another good reason for tourists to return to this island year after year. Aside from their reputation as a very friendly group of people, the locals of the "Garden Isle" are known to be athletic, artistic, and expressive. Other than these, they are also a loyal and intelligent group of people who are willing to put themselves in danger just to protect their island home from overdevelopment.

Common traits

The people of Kauai are considered as one of the friendliest people in all of the Hawaiian Islands, and this is not just a matter of opinion that most Kauai natives have of themselves. The natives of the island have actually been voted the friendliest by the Conde Nast Readers Choice Awards, from a survey that is conducted every year.

New and old visitors alike warm up to the sunny dispositions of its locals, despite the fact that rainy days are not uncommon in Kauai. Despite its reputation as one of the wettest places on earth, the island makes do with other activities to thrill and entertain guests even as the rain pours. Being hospitable hosts is one of them. Although guests are expected to remove their shoes before entering any Kauai home, the same home is always prepared to look after guests with good food and entertainment.

The people of Kauai are also known for their excellent stewardship of the island, remaining vigilant for any signs of modernization that could potentially lead to the exploitation of their island home. A typical example was the ruckus created by Kauai natives against a Superferry docking on its shores. The vessel, a military spec transport ship, is capable of carrying up to 800 people to the island at a time. Kauai natives held such a high objection to the vessel coming to its shores. There was an instance when Kauai surfers prevented the ferry from docking, forcing it to make its way back to Honolulu. Kauai natives avoided being branded as a group of xenophobic island people after this incident by making themselves clear. They said that the ferry violated environmental impact rules, did not follow regulations, and must not be allowed to set foot on the island.

The island is inhabited by about 58,000 people, a majority of which are of Asian origin. The rest is more or less the same proportion to native Hawaiians, Alaskans, and American Indians. This has resulted in the unique multi-cultural atmosphere that sustains locals. The same atmosphere is enjoyed by visitors from all over the world, with added flavor coming from the influx of musicians, artists, and other colorful personalities who simply want to make the island their home. Indeed, the island always comes alive with musical presentations on the beach or at museums and art exhibits by local artists.

Because of the island's location amidst lush tropical vegetation and craggy mountains overlooking crystal waters and prime surfing spots, the natives of Kauai are naturally active people who view surfing and hiking as part of their normal, everyday activities. Although Kauai locals love their food and there is plenty to go around, gaining weight has never been a problem when they can easily catch some waves or take a short hike to enjoy the island's scenery after a long sumptuous Polynesian meal. Even the simple activity of beachcombing in Larsen's Beach is enough to keep a few unwanted pounds at bay.

History

The people of Kauai came from the Marquesas and other Polynesian islands about 1,500 years ago. The Marquesans brought with them traditional food crops, including taro, which is now used to make Poi, a typical Kauai delicacy. Tahitians discovered the island about 1,000 AD. and overpowered the Marquesans, driving them off to other islands. The early settlers are responsible for the diverse plant life found on the island. Westerners started to arrive on the island during the 1700s, with the most famous of them being Captain James Cook who arrived with his two ships, the HMS Discovery and Revolution. Merchants and missionaries soon made their way after Western traders made their holds on the island.

Most of the island's people descended from the immigrants that came in waves during the birth of the sugar industry in Kauai, specifically in the district of Koloa in 1835. Immigrants from Japan, China, the Philippines, Portugal, Puerto Rico, Spain, and Germany, among other countries, flooded to the island in search of an idyllic life among the palm trees and pristine beaches of the Garden Isle. This rich infusion of cultures, traditions, and history has resulted in the colorful cultural mosaic. In recent years, the island has become one of the most desirable places to live since it was opened to the public as a prime tourist destination in the 1990s.

Despite becoming a US territory in the 1900s and attaining its statehood on August 21, 1959, natives of the Garden Isle have kept the spirit of independence that has made them unique from all the natives of the other Hawaiian islands.

Kauai's little people

The island is known for its legend of little people, known as the Menehune. Locals believe that the Menehunes were the island's earliest settlers and were believed to have worked at night to accomplish some of the amazing structures, most often stunning stonework, found all throughout the island. However, archaeologists believe that the Menehunes were actually not a mere legend but real people who once lived in Kauai. The Menehunes were said to have come from the Marquesas Islands and were already living in Hawaii long before the Tahitians arrived at the islands some time between 0 and 350 AD. Because the Polynesians were more war-like than the Menehunes, they were able to drive out the Menehunes north through the chain of other Hawaiian islands. Experts also believe that the word "Menehune" does not literally refer to a group of people with a characteristic of short stature, but people who were considered to belong to a lower caste.

The Menehunes were considered expert rock builders, although they did not use mortar in their projects. A good example of their creations in the island is the Menehune Ditch, which snakes along the Waimea River. The ditch is accessible from Highway 50 and inland to Menehune Road in Waimea. Another example of their legendary creations is the Menehune Fishpond on the Nawiliwili Harbor, which consists of stonework that used to span 25 miles. According to a legend, the fishpond was created in just one night, with thousands of the little creatures passing stones one by one. The fishpond is accessible on foot or by paddling up the Huleia Stream on a canoe. Hikers can walk from Nawiliwili Harbor up to Hulemalu Road. A marker will lead intrepid visitors to the fishpond.

The spirit of aloha

The people of Kauai live according to the spirit of aloha, the spirit that makes the island warm, friendly, and welcoming even to strangers. First-time guests will find it a pleasant surprise to see natives and locals who are always ready with a smile or a wave when they see guests on the road or anywhere else on the island. The readiness of the people to wave, smile, give a helping hand, or make way for guests on the road are proofs that Kauai natives take the aloha spirit to heart, which is not merely doing to others what they want to be done to them. As what Reverend Abraham Akaka said during the island's statehood celebration, the Golden Rule is aloha. "It is welcoming the stranger and seeking his or her good, loving a stranger even if love is not returned."

This spirit is felt warmly by tourists from all over the world. Those who were fortunate enough to make friends and find a second family among locals promise to come back to the island year after year. Aside from exploring the depths of Kauai's natural beauty, some tourists also take some time off the city life to seek refuge in the laid-back atmosphere of living in this island. Their vacation are not only spent taking a hike to different tourist destinations but also in celebrating important events with the locals and other tourists that help preserve its culture. The colorful festivals show much of the island people's cultural tradition. The festival celebrations alone will prove how artistic and expressive locals are, making this island a haven for some musicians, painters, and artists. They get inspiration from Kauai's beautiful landscapes and panorama, as well as from its laid-back, nature-loving people.

These people are not only known to express love and show respect to one another but also to nature. They consider Kauai not only as a world renowned tourist destination, but a blessing from nature as well. For this reason, they have fought hard to preserve its natural wonders and cultural heritage, despite threats of modernization.

The goodness of their hearts mirrors the pristine beauty of this island.

Kauai Festivals & Events

What makes a festival on Kauai so much fun for malihini (visitors) and kamaaina (residents)? Well, they have interesting cultural themes, there's always good food and good music, shopping is varied and reasonable, they're easy to find, and there's entertainment and activities for children too. And of course, there's plenty of aloha for everyone!

Kauai's multicultural population, history, and native flora and fauna contribute themes that are lively, interesting and educational. Kauai Festivals often include native Hawaiian ceremonies, concerts featuring traditional and contemporary music, lei making contests, and hula demonstrations. The themes of our festivals vary greatly and include reenactments of historic Hawaiian events, town celebrations, art shows, and events honoring each of the many diverse cultures still thriving on Kauai today. Kauai Festivals occur year-round and island-wide, and offer visitors the opportunity to explore our island and discover what makes Kauai truly unique among the islands of Hawaii.

Island Flavors Abound at Festivals
Key to every event's success is the great selection of ono grinds (delicious food) that can be found at all of Kauai's festivals. Sample favorite island foods at very reasonable prices, from standard outdoor fare like hamburgers and corn dogs, to "local" dishes including Hawaiian, Japanese, Filipino, Puerto Rican and Portuguese cuisine. Annual culinary events showcase Hawaii's fine seafood and produce, and the talents of our island chefs.

Join the Fun!
Kauai Festivals are not staged exhibitions. They are genuine community gatherings that bring together old friends and new to enjoy each other's company, to share food and to enjoy local music and culture. Admission to festivals and fairs is free or usually minimal, so families can enjoy the day or evening together. All ages are welcome and encouraged to attend.

Tourism

Kauai is the oldest island in Hawaii and is a twenty-minute flight from Honolulu. The tropical paradise was formed six million years ago and encompasses 550 miles with a population of approximately 60 000 people. Kauai lies in the azure blue waters of the Pacific Ocean and is the northernmost of the main Hawaiian Islands.

Appropriately nicknamed the Garden Isle, it is renowned for its flourishing greenery and post card perfect beauty. Kauai's magnificence is exceptionally significant that it has been an ideal setting for several Hollywood Productions including Jurassic Park. With verdant rainforests, angelic white sand kissing the sapphire ocean, breathtaking waterfalls, spectacular desert land and majestic mountains all under the same gypsy sun - the island boasts all of Mother Nature's glorious spectrum.

Enjoy not only the natural surroundings, but the island's vibrant range of cultures, attractions, activities, sports, shopping and dining. A visit to Kauai will exceed any dreams you have had about the perfect holiday destination. It offers all you need and beyond to experience a relaxing and enriching vacation that you will never forget. With a wide range of accommodation, you will easily be able to find the ultimate place for you to stay.

Aloha welcome to the closest thing to heaven and we invite you to come discover it, right here in Kauai, Hawaii.

What Makes Kauai Unique

If there's something that makes Kauai unique, it's the fact that everything Hawaiian can be found in the islands. From its rich history, geology, culture, and sights, you can get a full view of what Hawaii is all about in Kauai. If you're asking for scenic beaches, Kauai has those. If you want wildlife and nature, Kauai has those aplenty. If you're looking for culture and history, Kauai is the best place to be. Whether it's for weddings, romantic getaways, seclusion, and memorable stays, just let Kauai take care of you. Want to give your swing a try? Golf courses are something that Kauai has a lot of. Everything that Hawaii stands for, is famous for, and is loved for, can be found in Kauai. Now if you're still asking what makes Kauai special, the next thing you need to do is to visit Kauai and see for yourself how Kauai stands for all things essentially Hawaiian.

The cradle of Hawaiian civilization

When it comes to Hawaii, nothing can beat the Kauai among the islands of Hawaii. Kauai is the point where the first settlers of Hawaii landed ashore, and one can even claim that Kauai is the foundation on which the Hawaiian nation and culture was built on. With artifacts as early as 200 AD being found on the island, when it comes to seniority in terms of being populated, Kauai brings home the trophy. You can call Kauai the cradle of the Hawaiian civilization.

And not only that, Kauai is also rich in folklores and songs about the Menehune, the theoretical Marquesans who were believed to be the first settlers of Kauai.

And how do you think Hawaii was discovered by Europeans? Of course, it was through Kauai. James Cook landed on the shores of Kauai, and it was from the Kauai Island that Hawaii became known to the rest of the world. And from this initial contact, the influx of western influence was started, drastically changing the face and destiny of the natives of Hawaii. Aside from the countless deaths caused by the diseases brought by western ships and their navigators, the arrival of the Europeans also signaled for the radical change in the Hawaiian belief system, from their native Tahitian religions to the

Christian religion that the western missionaries brought to the Kauaian shores.

But before those things occurred, it was Kauai that formed the last obstacle to the unification of Hawaii under a single rule. But through negotiations, a peaceful surrender was made by the ruler of Kauai to Kamehameha I, indirectly contributing to the establishment of the first unified nation of Hawaii, the Kingdom of Hawaii.

Rich native Hawaiian culture with Asian and Western influences

In terms of culture, you're sure to find a lot of it in Kauai. As you know, history and culture go together, and with the rich history of Kauai, you can also find culture in abundance. From the artifacts and temples that the ancient Hawaiians left, to the plantations, museums, churches, and lighthouses that the western influence has brought to Hawaii, you can find them all in Kauai. Whether it's ancient, contemporary, or modern culture, Kauai stands as one of the chief cultural centers of the state. Aside from historic influences, you can also find several art galleries and artist colonies in Kauai. These colonies and art centers preserve the rich cultural tradition of Hawaii. Whether it's visual art, music, or the performing arts, you should find that Kauai has those in abundance. Aside from the museums, you can also find state national parks that give information about the ancient culture of Hawaii, especially the Polihale State Park and the Prince Kuhio Park where you can get a first-hand experience of Hawaiian culture. Aside from that, you also get to know some of the local folklores and legends surrounding Kauai by visiting historic places and landmarks in this island.

Plantations and the tourism industry

Another thing that stands out in Kauai is the plantations that brought economic prosperity to the island. The first plantation industry in Kauai was that of sugar, and it was highly successful, with the industry lasting for many decades. Due to the capitalistic tendencies of the foreign settlers, the rich, fertile land of Kauai was utilized to create sugar plantations that put Kauai and Hawaii in the economic map of the world. Even until today, you can still see sugar plantations in Kauai and the remnants of the railroads and mills of the sugar plantations of the previous century.

Another thing that is unique to Kauai is being the melting pot of several cultures from different nations. As the previous endemic of western diseases reduced the number of native Hawaiians significantly, along with the increased demand for labor in the plantations, a need for extra labor surfaced. Because of this, the influx of immigrants in Hawaii was initiated. The plantations called forth laborers and workers from different nations, such as Japan, China, Philippines, Puerto Rico, and Portugal. The result is the mixed race make-up of the present population of modern Hawaii. You can also now find that these laborers brought with them their own cultures and integrated them with Hawaii's native one. As such, the culture of Hawaii and its islands was further enriched due to the contribution of these modern immigrants.

Next to the sugar plantations are the pineapple plantations. Pineapple canning and plantations gained success, but not of the same magnitude as the sugar plantations did. The pineapple plantations in Kauai experienced about half a century of prosperity before closing shop in the 1960s. The previous canning factories and plantations now are the sites of resorts and other tourism businesses.

And that brings us to one of the main industries in Kauai, which is tourism. As mentioned earlier, the appeal of Kauai is that it has all things essentially Hawaiian, thus becoming a top tourist spot in Hawaii. Offering all the rich culture, history, and natural resources of Hawaii in a single island, Kauai is the place to go when one wants to know the Hawaiian spirit. At present, the tourism industry accounts for a significant percentage of the revenue of the County of Kauai. This presented the county of Kauai with plenty of jobs, and revenues and opportunities for small and large businesses.

Scenery and natural wildlife

Another feature of Kauai that makes it unique is the natural beauty of its surroundings and the rich plant and animal life that it hosts on its island. The valleys, crags, mountains, and canyons in Kauai present some of the most majestic views in Hawaii.

Of course, you have the dozens of beaches that line the shores of Kauai. From the white beaches of Salt Pond Beach to the golden-brown sands of the Royal Coconut Coast, Kauai has a lot of beautiful and scenic beaches to offer. These beaches also serve as venues for all kinds of water activities and entertainment; you can go snorkeling, scuba diving, surfing, body boarding, and swimming in the pristine waters of this tropical island.

Aside from that, these beaches also form a great part of the views in the championship level golf courses that Kauai has. The Kauai Lagoons Golf Club and Princeville Golf Course are golf courses that have held PGA Tournaments in the past, and are well-rated for their challenge, great design, and spectacular views of the Pacific coast and the lush vegetation of the tropical rainforests, and the towering mountains of inland Kauai.

You can find Waimea Canyon in Kauai. Waimea Canyon is one deep, large, and panoramic view of the Kauai landscape. Because of the grand view that it provides, the Waimea Canyon has also been called the Grand Canyon of the Pacific. You can also find several valleys and waterfalls in Kauai. The most noted of the valleys is the one in Wailua, where Hawaiian nobility go to when giving birth to their offspring, with the belief that this valley provides the blessings of the gods. As for waterfalls, you can look for the Kipu Falls, Wailua Falls, and the Opaeka'a Falls for a great photo opportunity.

As for animal and plant life, you can find several migratory and native birds along the East and Na Pali Coast, as well as an abundance of marine life such as humpback whales, dolphins, and monk seals on the island's south and west coasts. There are also several state natural parks in the island to give you a guided tour of the natural surroundings, and be informed of the conservation efforts that are made towards the preservation of local wildlife. As Hawaii is also called the Endangered Species Capital of the World, you can get a lot of information about how endangered species are protected and preserved from extinction. This also makes Kauai a great family vacation destination and a good venue for children to learn about the importance of nature and the protection of natural wildlife.

Kauai is unique
All of these things are what make Kauai one of the exceptional islands in Hawaii, and perhaps the world. Its great combination of natural

beauty, wildlife, and rich history and culture results to something that can only be found in Kauai.

Tourist Attractions and Festivals in Kauai

The island of Kauai is a place of colorful festivals and interesting sights and attractions. This tropical destination is known for its untouched nature, majestic canyons, and volcanic craters, as well as various tourist attractions in the form of old buildings, monuments, and a host of diverse activities to keep visitors occupied.

Popular Kauai festivals

Kauai is not called the island of festivals for no reason at all. It celebrates a number of festivals all-year round, among them are the annual Kauai Mokihana Festival, the Hawaii International Film Festival, and the famous May Day, or Lei Day. The annual Kauai Mokihana Festival is an eight-day affair, featuring the island's most famous artists and musicians. There are presentations on natural healing, as well as slack key guitar tutorials.

In February, the island comes alive with the sporting spirit from the 5-km and 10-km fun run, also known as Captain Cook's Caper. Aside from this, sporting events held during the Waimea Town Celebration also include the outrigger canoe race. The town is known for its many festivals and celebrations all-year round, among them are the popular song fests in February that last for ten weeks.

May Day, more commonly known as Lei Day, is a springtime celebration of the island's diverse flora. Aside from lei-making competitions, different museum exhibits also mark the celebration of this event. In June, you can be part of one of the most famous culinary festivals in the island, the Taste of Hawaii. This event by Kapaa Rotary Club brings together traditional food and mouth-watering dishes prepared by chefs from all over the islands. The O Bon Season also starts in June. This is a festival that celebrates the arrival of Japanese immigrants to the island. The highlight of the celebration is the lighting of tiny Japanese paper boats that are then sent out to sea. June also marks the celebration of the birth of Kamameha the Great, following the Koloa Plantation Days in July.

In August, the island prepares for the Kauai-Tahiti Fete, which features dancers from all over Hawaii, Tahiti, Canada, and the other islands. The Aloha Week Festival is celebrated every October, with dance, music, and traditional Hawaiian food as among the top attractions.

The Hawaii International Film festival is one thing to look forward to in November. Locals and tourists alike can watch the best of Pacific Rim films for free in various island theaters. Tourists have another good reason to extend their stay till December, when island craft artists, painters, and makers of traditional Hawaiian art exhibit their works during the craft fair. The island also comes to life because of its tropical Christmas spirit, with the formation of yearly choral groups and musical ensembles, as well as youth drama groups.

Other attractions

The island is also host to a number of attractions that draw crowds of tourists and locals alike. A popular example is the "Surf to Sunset" luau of Sheraton Kauai Resort, which is set just footsteps from the Poipu Beach. It features a myriad of Hawaiian entertainment, drinks, and food. The banquet is a mix of traditional Hawaiian and international food, from fresh fruits to Japanese, Chinese, Vietnamese, Filipino, and Thai delicacies, which can be served family or buffet style. All these gustatory delights can be enjoyed while listening to traditional Hawaiian performers and watching the Hula dancers sway in the background.

Another attraction is the Grand Hyatt Kauai Luau, which is famous for sumptuous banquets amidst the best Polynesian and Hawaiian entertainment the island can offer. This includes ancient Kahiko Hula and the pulsating beats of traditional Tahitian dances. A particular crowd pleaser is the enchanting knife dance performed by local

Hawaiian entertainers. Guests can expect to be greeted by warm shell lei greetings before settling for the Hawaiian buffet.

Yet another famous attraction is the Smith's Garden Luau. This luau features the traditional Hawaiian pa'ina or feast, the central attraction in any luau. The buffet also features the traditional Hawaiian dishes of roasted Kalua pig, ono mahimahi, and chicken adobo. Diners are also welcome to practice a few Hula moves after dinner, as the luau crew serenades them with traditional Hula music and Hawaiian chanting.

Kauai activities

After a sumptuous meal, you have a lot of things to keep yourself busy on the island. Aside from hiking, trekking, and engaging in one of the many watersports and activities, you can also take a daytrip to one of the neighboring islands by Hawaiian Airines, which offers safe day trips at cheap rates.

You can also take a closer look at the deepest canyon in the Pacific, the Waimea Canyon, which played a role in the hit Speilberg flick, "Jurassic Park." The diverse marine life is also a major attraction here in Kauai, especially for divers from all over the world. Kauai is also known for Koloa Landing, one of the most awesome dive sites in the island. Divers regularly get to meet Hawaiian green sea turtles and monk seals in this dive spot.

The main attraction of the island is its rural, uncommercialized nature. The sandy beaches here are as captivating as those found on postcards, which all seem untouched. Basic necessities are available from the mom and pop stores that dot the island, while upscale comforts are not too far away, with the many three- or four-star hotels and resorts all within a short walking or driving distance.

Tourist spots

The Garden Isle will not cease to amaze visitors with its treasure trove of natural wonders, even as they go deeper into the interior. Those looking for a bit of history can head over to the Old Koloa Town, located on the South Shore, where they can get a glimpse of the architectural history of the island. This is also the location of the Kauai Coffee Company, which is now one of the largest coffee producers in the US. Another equally interesting attraction is the Alekoko Fishponds where visitors can listen to the legend of the Menehune, little people who built the fishponds thousands of years ago. Another interesting stop is the Kilauea Point, where they can see the Hanalei Church and the Kauai Lighthouse.

Another place of interest is the Grove Farm Homestead Museum, as well as the Huleia National Wildlife Refuge, one of the places where the opening scenes of the "Raiders of the Lost Ark" were filmed. You can also visit Captain Cook's Monument located in the rural town of Hofgaard Park, which is where Captain Cook first landed in 1778. Captain Cook, along with the crew of the Discovery and the Resolution, is the first Westerner to set foot on the islands.

Another interesting historical point is the Russian Fort Elizabeth, named after Russian doctor Georg Scheffer. He was able to persuade the Hawaiian king to build a fort near Waimea. Other forts were erected near Hanalei. Unfortunately, the Russian doctor could not remain on the island without the backing of the Russian czar, and so, he was forced to leave his forts. This is the only remaining fort in Hawaii.

Other natural attractions in the island include its many beaches, most of them secluded and devoid of the throngs of tourists that characterize other Hawaiian island resorts. Popular beaches include Salt Pond Beach, Shipwreck Beach, and Poipu Beach. More beautiful beaches can be found on the North Shore, which includes the Kee, Hanalei, and Secret Beaches.

For those who want to take a look at secluded beaches that are not easily accessible to most visitors, they can hike their way up to Honopu Beach, where one of the famous scenes of "King Kong" with

Jessica Lange was filmed. They can also take a hike at Kalalau Valley, which opens to the Hanea State Park that sits on Wainiha Bay.

For a unique perspective of the Garden Isle, you can take a helicopter tour that allows you to see the Tunnel of Eucalyptus Trees, the Waita Reservoir, Captain Cook's Landing, and Lumahai Beach, all from above. Helicopter tours can last for an hour. Another interesting alternative is the helicopter kayak combo tour, which gives visitors the opportunity to take a glimpse of the Mt. Wai'ale'ale with its many waterfalls. Guests are given time to enjoy the water. They must bring with them swimming gear and ample sun protection. There is also the Kauai Custom Flight, a 65–minute narrated tour, which covers a majority of the island's most popular attractions.

Whale watching is an added treat in winter. Other points of interest include Kipu Kai, Hanapepe Valley, and the Na Pali coastline. Other guests may prefer the Kauai Grand Flight, which takes 70 minutes to cover nine prime tourist spots including Kipu Kai, Hanapepe Valley, Olokeke Canyon, the Waimea Canyon, the Wailua Waterfall, and Princeville. Another popular tour is the Kalapaki Bay Kayak Tour, an ideal tour for kayaking beginners.

Their colorful festivals and fun-filled celebrations all add up to reasons you should rediscover Kauai and enjoy the many tourist attractions and activities this island has to offer.

Activities and Attractions

Biking

Kauai Road and Mountain Biking

There are lots of options for renting bicycles on the east side. The Ke Ala Hele Makalae Kapaa bike path starts at Lihi Park in Kapaa and follows the coast north, ending at Ahihi Point, just past Donkey Beach. There is also a 2.5 mile section at Lydgate Beach Park which will eventually connect with the Kapaa section when construction is completed. This incredible path is available to walkers, joggers, roller bladders, bikers, and is safe for families and strollers. The bike path meanders along the ocean for several miles. Cruise along with great views of the Pacific, see whales breaching and spouting late fall and during winter, stop for a bite to eat or take a dip in the ocean. Rent your own bike or enjoy a guided trip.

For the more adventurous bikers, there are several trails in the area that are open to mountain biking. Enjoy the ocean views and the rush of winding down a jungle mountain. Shops can point you in the right

Boat Tours

Take a Kauai Boat Tour

One of the main attractions on the Royal Coconut Coast are boat tours. The prime destination along the Wailua River is the Fern Grotto. This amazing natural lava rock grotto used to be reserved exclusively for the royalty of Hawaii. Now it welcomes guests and has become a popular wedding venue for locals and visitors alike. Open-air boats offer a great platform to get to the grotto; you will be entertained by hula dancers and chanters telling the stories and legends of the area.

The prime destination along the Wailua River is the Fern Grotto.

While not on the Royal Coconut Coast, the Napali Coast is a spectacular site not to be missed on Kauai. Staying on the Royal Coconut Coast ensures that you are never far from everything Kauai has to offer. A short drive away and you will find many companies and vessel options for exploring the Napali Coast by boat. Napali means "the cliffs" or "many cliffs" and you will see why very quickly. It features incredible 4,000 foot cliffs that stretch right into the ocean. Sea caves and waterfalls create picture-perfect settings everywhere you look.

Fishing on Kauai is a profitable venture for some and a long-time hobby for others. Many ancient traditions are still practiced to find the best fishing spot for the day. Join others or charter a boat to try your hand at fishing the fresh or ocean waters of Kauai. Deep sea fishing can be a real thrill, often finding large fish such as marlins, tuna, and wahoo. Most fishing adventures let you keep a portion of your catch so you can cook it up and taste your well-earned rewards.

Health & Rejuvenation

Health & Rejuvenation

Interested in the healing powers of ocean therapy, relieving stress or relaxing in lush, peaceful surroundings? Want to be pampered with facials, massages and bodywork? Can you imagine massage next to the ocean or learning how the natural elements can heal? Want to feel rejuvenated while enjoying the tranquility and peace of Kauai's extraordinary environment? The Royal Coconut Coast offers exceptional personal care, health treatments and education in local spas and wellness centers. Locally owned and staffed by highly trained therapists, the choices of therapy and treatments include Hawaiian techniques passed down through many generations. Plan a session at one of the east side's exceptional spa and treatment centers.

Hiking

Hiking on the Royal Coconut Coast

Hiking is an incredible way to experience the island and see beautiful interior landscapes of mountains and waterfalls. Imagine life before civilization as you trek deep into the jungle, and experience the islands natural splendor. A variety of hiking is available; there are kid-friendly trails as well as challenging trails that traverse mountains and streams. Pick up a guide book so you can easily spot and identify native wildlife, flora and fauna.

Trails are identified with signs and well maintained. Trail maps are available through the Department of Land and Natural Resources and the Division of State Parks. Always be sure to pack plenty of water and snacks, even if only venturing a short distance. Avoid hiking alone, but if you do always tell someone where you are going and when you expect to return. Do not drink untreated water from streams.

AN IMPORTANT NOTE ABOUT CAMPING ON KAUAI

Camping on the Island of Kauai is only allowed at select State and County parks and camping at either type of park requires that you obtain a permit. While these permits are very affordable, the fine for camping without one can be as high as $500.

Horseback Tours

Kauai Horseback Tours

Enjoy the sounds of nature and breathtaking views of the island from horseback. Horseback riding tours are a popular option for those wanting to see hidden landscapes of Kauai and experience a little adventure. Guided tours are available for all skill levels, from beginners to advanced, so the whole family can enjoy. Many different settings are available whether you prefer to ride on the beach or into the interior jungles of the Garden Isle. Ride along ocean bluffs, through sugar cane fields, and even journey to private waterfalls where you can enjoy a refreshing swim. Tours range from 90 minutes to all day adventures with an experienced guide that will show you the way, share history and legends of the area, provide knowledge of local flora and fauna, and supply the refreshments. Put your jeans on and step back in time, enjoy Kauai the way the paniolo (Hawaiian cowboy) do.

Luau

Experience a Kauai Luau on the Coconut Coast
A luau is a tradition every visitor should partake to experience and learn more about Hawaiian cultures and customs. Most luau feature an incredible buffet and variety of foods, but the highlight of a traditional luau is the kalua pork or roasted pig. The pig is often cooked all day or overnight in an imu, an underground oven full of hot

coals and lava rocks. The pig is covered and sealed, and cooks for hours until it is soft.

A typical luau not only offers an endless buffet of delicious foods, but also a chance to try a mai tai or other tropical drinks. A mai tai usually consists of fresh island juices like pineapple, guava, passion fruit, and lime with light and dark rums. Another island favorite is a lava flow, which is basically a pina coloda with a swirl of strawberry syrup that makes a sweet and stylish drink. Other locally made spirits have become quite popular, Kauai now features its own rum and fruit wines that are made on island.

Guests at a luau get to enjoy dinner and a show. Most luau consists of a variety of entertainment. Hula and Tahitian dancing, along with fire dancing and chanting are the highlights for most people. Experience the true spirit of aloha and take a journey through time with songs and dance from ancient peoples.

Surfing & Stand Up Paddling

There are several great beaches and areas for surfers of all skill levels to enjoy. If you are a beginner, sign up for a surf lesson to learn how to ride the waves of Kauai. If you are experienced, rent a board and enjoy some of the best waves in the world. Surfing can be a real rush, those who try it once often end up going back for more.

Stand-up paddling is the newest craze sweeping the island, a fun way to get on a board for the first time. Stand-up paddle boards are bigger and wider than most surf boards, allowing almost anyone to be able to stand up with ease. You are given a paddle to navigate your way through the water and try to catch waves if you are brave enough. The Wailua River offers a great place to try stand-up paddling for the first time, with no waves or currents; you can get the feel for it before venturing into the ocean

Ziplining on Kauai

Capture a bird's eye view of Kauai while soaring at up to 35-miles an hour above its lush valleys, streams and rain forests on an exhilarating zipline tour. These eco-friendly tours will provide you with both a thrilling experience and educational insight into Kauai's rich history.

Enjoy the rush as you soar above a green jungle canopy, 50-80 feet above the ground. Panoramic views surround you as you descend into the forest below. You'll also learn about Kauai's diverse ecosystem filled with rare endemic plant and animal species.

Kauai is home to a variety of ziplining opportunities, each offering a unique aerial perspective of the island's diverse landscapes. Princeville Ranch Adventures (North Shore), Kauai Backcountry Adventures and Just Live (Lihue), as well as Outfitters Kauai (South Shore) all operate zipline courses. All zipline companies will have similar requirements and restrictions. For tour-specific information, please contact each zipline company directly.

Whale Watching on Kauai

From December to May, you are likely to catch a glimpse of a majestic kohola, or humpback whale, off Kauai's shorelines. These gentle giants come to the warm Hawaiian waters every year to breed and give birth to new calves.

Schedule a tour or charter a boat to spot these magnificent creatures. Treat yourself to scenic ocean views as guides take you to the best spots to observe whales playfully surfacing, tail slapping, or blowing spouts in the air. Regulations prohibit boats from approaching within 100 yards of a whale and you should never swim with or touch whales or any other marine animals.

You can also spot whales from Kauai's many beautiful beaches, including Poipu Beach on the South Shore, and from scenic spots like

Kilauea Lighthouse and the Napali Coast's Kalalau Trail on the North Shore. On the East Side, the Kapaa Overlook between Kapaa Town and Kealia Beach is another notable viewing spot. Whales are attracted to Hawaii's warm, shallow waters, so keep your eyes open on the sands of Kauai.

Snorkeling and Scuba on Kauai

As amazing as this island is on land, you'll discover even more incredible sights in the waters of Kauai. While flourishing gardens and rainforests get most of the attention on Kauai, the island offers a wide range of snorkeling and scuba spots to explore under the sea.

On the North Shore, fantastic shoreline snorkeling beaches include the reefs off Kee Beach and Haena Beach Park. Anini Beach offers a lagoon great for beginning snorkelers. Makua, or "Tunnels," Beach in Haena also has a wide reef area that's a treat to the senses.

On the East Side, Lydgate Beach Park offers a protected snorkeling lagoon great for keiki (children) snorkelers.

On the South Shore, Poipu Beach State Park offers protected areas for snorkelers. Be sure to check ocean conditions and currents prior to going out, especially during the big north shore swells of the winter.

Scuba

Kauai also offers a variety of scuba sites for beginners and experienced divers. Dive tours offer plenty of tropical fish, reef creatures, dolphins and honu (Hawaiian Green Sea Turtles) to discover. Experienced divers will generally find more thrilling spots on the east and west shores, including cave exploration and lava tubes.

Those new to scuba should start on the north or south shores (Hanalei, Kee Beach, or Poipu Beach).

You can rent all the necessary gear and equipment on Kauai, as well as get your certification on the island, but bring your medical paperwork with you if you choose to get certified. Also, keep in mind that if you drive to Waimea Canyon or Kokee State Park, or want to take a helicopter excursion, you need to wait 24-hours due to altitude change.

Kauai Gardens & Parks

Kauai is known as "The Garden Isle" for its tropical rainforests, fertile valleys and lush flora. So it's not surprising to find some of Hawaii's most beautiful botanical gardens on Kauai. You can find three of the nation's five National Tropical Botanical Gardens on Kauai: the Allerton Garden and McBryde Garden on the South Shore, and Limahuli Gardens in Haena. McBryde Garden is home to the largest collection of native Hawaiian flora in the world, while Allerton Gardens features amazing landscaping and the giant Moreton Figs made famous in the film "Jurassic Park." The 17-acre Limahuli Gardens offers endangered native plants, taro-filled agricultural terraces and beautiful views of the North Shore.

Other botanical gardens and plantations include Na Aina Kai Botanical Gardens, Smith's Tropical Paradise Botanical Garden and the Kauai Coffee Plantation. You can also take a tour of Hanalei's taro farms to learn about this versatile Hawaiian root starch.

Kayaking on Kauai

Kauai is home to the only navigable rivers in Hawaii, so kayaking is an integral part of a unique Kauai vacation.

Relax and take in the exquisite scenery as you paddle down the Wailua River. This popular river for kayaking weaves by lush, jungle landscapes along with island's East Side. Other river routes include the Huleia River from Nawiliwili Harbor in Lihue, as well as the Hanalei River on the North Shore, the longest on the island.

If you're up for a more difficult challenge, ocean kayaking is a seasonal alternative to experience Kauai by sea. On the South Shore, try the Poipu to Port Allen course with a stop in Lawai Bay. When conditions are calm, kayaking along the 17-mile Napali Coast is unforgettable. "National Geographic" deemed kayaking the Napali Coast the second best adventure in the country. Because this can be a physically demanding activity and the seas can be unpredictable, hiring a guide for this once-in-a-lifetime experience is a must

Hula on Kauai

Get a glimpse of Hawaii's thriving hula tradition during your visit to Kauai. The dance, accompanied by a chant or percussive elements, preserves the traditions and culture of Hawaii. Hula has a special meaning to Kauai, as the island's legends suggest that the art form began on its shores. At Keahualaka on the Napali Coast, a fabled Hawaiian love story unfolded. When Lohiau, a handsome mortal Kauai chief, danced before the volcano goddess Pele, the two fell passionately in love. Today, hula dancers still come to this sacred spot to demonstrate their skills.

You can see hula on Kauai at seasonal festivals, events, competitions, live performances and luau (although the latter often mixes traditional Hawaiian dances with those of other Polynesian cultures). Hula is taught by a kumu hula (hula teacher) in a halau hula (hula school), but visitors can take free hula lessons offered at various locations around Kauai, including some hotels and resorts.

Kauai has many fantastic luau venues where you can watch hula performances and learn more about Polynesian and Hawaiian cultures, including the Grand Hyatt Kauai Luau at the Grand Hyatt Kauai Resort and Spa on the South Shore. Or check out the Smith Family Garden Luau in Kapaa and the Luau Kalamaku in the historic Kilohana Plantation.

Whale Watching on Kauai

From December to May, you are likely to catch a glimpse of a majestic kohola, or humpback whale, off Kauai's shorelines. These gentle giants come to the warm Hawaiian waters every year to breed and give birth to new calves.

Schedule a tour or charter a boat to spot these magnificent creatures. Treat yourself to scenic ocean views as guides take you to the best spots to observe whales playfully surfacing, tail slapping, or blowing spouts in the air. Regulations prohibit boats from approaching within 100 yards of a whale and you should never swim with or touch whales or any other marine animals.

You can also spot whales from Kauai's many beautiful beaches, including Poipu Beach on the South Shore, and from scenic spots like Kilauea Lighthouse and the Napali Coast's Kalalau Trail on the North

Shore. On the East Side, the Kapaa Overlook between Kapaa Town and Kealia Beach is another notable viewing spot. Whales are attracted to Hawaii's warm, shallow waters, so keep your eyes open on the sands of Kauai.

Kauai's Scenic Byways

The island of Kauai is the oldest and northernmost of the eight major islands in the archipelago, making it the first island sighted by Captain Cook in 1778 and Captain Vancouver in 1792. Graced with time-worn cliffs and lush rainforests, the Garden Isle is filled with miles of roads to explore and stories waiting to be told.

Holo Holo Koloa Scenic Byway

In Hawaiian, the term *holo holo* means to go for a drive or a ride, so if your travels take you on the 19.5-mile Holo Holo Koloa Scenic Byway, you know it was meant to be. This story begins on the Maluhia Road with a magical passage through a tree tunnel that transports you into the old sugar plantation town of Koloa, and even further back into time to a recently discovered ancient Hawaiian village named Kaneiolouma Heiau. You'll also discover salt ponds, world-class Poipu Beach, a sacred hula mound named Pau a Laka and National Tropical Botanical Garden with the largest collection of endangered plant species in the world, as well as many other historically significant sites.

Kauai Restaurants & Food on the Coconut Coast

Kauai may be a small island, but there is nothing small about the culinary offerings available. Kauai is influenced from people and cultures all over the world, and that has translated onto the dinner plate. Many eateries feature a fusion of flavors from all over the world, with a tropical twist. With many small farms around the island, most Kauai dining establishments take advantage of the incredible variety of fresh, local produce available. Different kinds of fresh fish can be found at almost any establishment, prepared in many signature styles.

The Royal Coconut Coast offers a great variety of restaurants and eateries for every budget.

Find local favorites like plate lunches or burgers. For cheap eats try the many food trucks parked near the ocean. Or opt for fine dining and enjoy a romantic dinner with an ocean view. Several fine dining establishments are available, most offering fresh, local meats and fish. Vegetarians and vegans can find many delicious options in the area. Numerous cultures are represented in food; you can find fantastic restaurants specializing in European, Italian, Indian, Mexican, Japanese, Thai, or Chinese, to name a few. The restauran

Historic Places of Kauai

Kauai is the oldest island in the Hawaiian chain, giving its people a strong appreciation for local history and culture. From Captain Cook's arrival in Waimea to the first sugar plantation in Koloa, take the time to explore Kauai's rich history.

Heritage Sites
Kauai has two Heritage Sites of Hawaii special places located throughout the islands that provide significant historical, cultural and environmental contributions to the understanding and enjoyment of the state. Waimea Canyon State Park, appropriately nicknamed "The Grand Canyon of the Pacific," stretches for 14 miles within Kauai's west side and offers breathtaking canyon panoramas and great hiking trails.

Meanwhile, the Daniel K. Inouye Kilauea Lighthouse at Kilauea Point National Wildlife Refuge rewards visitors with amazing views of the Pacific Ocean and the Kauai's rugged north coast.

Small Towns
Kauai also has many small towns with historical significance. In 1778, British explorer Captain James Cook landed in Hawaii for the first time in Waimea Town. He named the paradise the "Sandwich Isles" after

the Earl of Sandwich and introduced Hawaii to the world. A statue of Cook now stands in Waimea Town to honor his discovery.

Just east of Waimea is Hanapepe Town. Once a thriving community in the mid-1900s, it's now Kauai's art capital. Even further west on the South Shore is Old Koloa Town. Home to Kauai's first sugar mill in 1835, an exploration of the Koloa Heritage Trail will give you insight into the history of Kauai and its multicultural population.

Museums

The island has many museums that allow you to see the Kauai of the past. In Hanalei Town, the Waioli Mission House and Waioli Huiia Church give you a glimpse of missionary life in the 1830s. North of Waimea Canyon is the Kokee Natural Museum in Kokee State Park, which offers an overview of the 4,345 acre park and the history of Waimea Canyon.

The 100-acre Grove Farm Homestead Museum in Lihue interprets how a sugar plantation worked in the 1860s. The Kauai Museum, also in Lihue, is the island's most important museum for preserving native Hawaiian artifacts and historical photos and showcasing the artists of Kauai.

Legendary Places

The people of Kauai have passed down early stories that live on in places you can still visit today. Near Lihue, visit Alekoko Fishpond and learn about the Menehune, Hawaii's "little people" who, according to the story, built this 1000-year-old pond in one night.

Legends also say that the hula began on the shores of Kauai. On the Napali Coast, the Ka Ulu o Laka heiau (temple) is a sacred spot where dancers still come to perform in honor of their strong hula traditions. Note: Heiau are sacred to the Hawaiian people and can be fragile and easily damaged. Do not climb over the rock walls, do not take anything from the sites (including stones) and treat them with great reverence and respect.

Waimea Canyon

What: On the southwest side of Kauai in Waimea

Where: Scenic canyon nicknamed "The Grand Canyon of the Pacific"

When: Open daily during daylight hours

How much: free admission

More Info: Parking lot, restrooms, lookout

Waimea Canyon, on Kauai's West Side, is described as "The Grand Canyon of the Pacific." Although not as big or as old as its Arizona cousin, you won't encounter anything like this geological wonder in

Hawaii. Stretching 14 miles long, 1 mile wide and more than 3,600 feet deep, the Waimea Canyon Lookout provides panoramic views of crested buttes, rugged crags and deep valley gorges. The grand inland vistas go on for miles.

The main road, Waimea Canyon Drive, leads you to a lower lookout point and the main Waimea Canyon Overlook, offering views of Kauai's dramatic interior. The road continues into the mountains and ends at Kokee State Park. There are numerous trails to traverse for beginners and seasoned hikers alike.

Daniel K. Inouye Kilauea Point Lighthouse

What: Beautiful views from Kauai's northernmost tip
Where: A 45-minute drive north of Lihue

Perched at the northernmost tip of Kauai, the 52-foot Daniel K. Inouye Kilauea Point Lighthouse was built in 1913 as a beacon for traveling ships. Although its light was turned off in the 1970s and has been replaced by an automatic beacon, it still serves as one of the island's most frequented attractions.

The view off the rugged northern coastline and the deep-blue Pacific makes this the perfect vantage point for photos. This is also the location of the Kilauea Point National Wildlife Refuge, a sanctuary for seabirds. Signage throughout the refuge identifies the area's bird species, including frigates, shearwaters, boobies and Laysan albatrosses nesting on the property. You'll see them soar the skies above the refuge, many landing on a small nearby island covered in birds. During December through May, you may even catch a glimpse of humpback whales. This scenic peninsula, 200-feet above sea level, is a must-see on your visit to the North Shore.

Tours are offered Wednesdays and Saturdays at 10:30 and 11:30 a.m. and at 12:30, 1:30 and 2:30 p.m. pending availability of staff or volunteers. Tour involves walking up steep, narrow steps. Restrictions: Children must be at least 44 inches tall. No infants. Backpacks, tripods and other large items are not allowed in the Kilauea Lighthouse.

Waimea Town

What: Historic seaport town

Where: In southwest Kauai, west of Hanapepe

On your way to Waimea Canyon, make a stop in Waimea Town on the West Side. This historic seaport town is a stone's throw from where British discoverer Captain James Cook first landed in Hawaii in 1778. A statue of Captain Cook can be found in the center of town, a replica of the original statue found in Whitby, England. Rich in paniolo history

(Hawaiian cowboys), this charming town is home to a variety of small shops and businesses as well as a growing number of tech companies.

While you're in Waimea Town, stop by the West Kauai Technology & Visitor Center, a great place to learn more about Kauai's past. The center features exhibits, programs and weekly activities that reflect the diversity of Kauai's agricultural community. Call for more information (registration is required for some events and programs). Along with Hanapepe, Waimea Town is an off-the-beaten-path discovery that's a great place to stop as you explore Kauai's West Side.

Hanapepe Town

What: Small town, art capital of Kauai

Where: Southwest Kauai, between Koloa and Waimea

Located on the south shore west of Koloa, Hanapepe Town once flourished as one of Kauai's largest communities. From World War I to the early 1950s, West Side Hanapepe was also one of Kauai's busiest towns, alive with G.I.s and sailors who were stationed there for training.

Today, "Kauai's biggest little town" hasn't changed much over the last century at first look. Its historic buildings are so authentic that the town was used as a location for films like "The Thornbirds" and "Flight of the Intruder," and even served as the model for the Disney film "Lilo and Stitch." But now those plantation-style buildings are home to charming shops, local eateries and more art galleries than any other spot on Kauai.

Hanapepe Town hosts a farmer's market on Thursdays starting at 3 p.m. And it celebrates its artists every Friday from 5-9 p.m., as painters, sculptors and craftsmen open the doors of their galleries and studios to celebrate the arts. Visit the galleries, take a walk on the "Hanapepe Swinging Bridge" which is always an adventure to cross then shop and dine in one of Kauai's most famous small towns.

Old Koloa Town

What: Charming town rooted in its plantation past

Where: About 20 minutes west from Lihue

Historic and picturesque, the Koloa district spans from Old Koloa Town to Kauai's beautiful South Shore in Poipu. Koloa opened its first sugar mill in 1835 and set the precedent for commercial sugar production across the islands. The sugar era opened the door to a wave of immigrants that make up Hawaii's multicultural population today.

The gateway to the Koloa/Poipu area is called the Tree Tunnel, a stretch of Maluhia Road lined with eucalyptus trees first planted a century ago. The Tree Tunnel still thrives and welcomes visitors today.

Old Koloa Town has retained much of its charm with shops now occupying the plantation buildings along Koloa Road. Stroll by old-fashioned storefronts and discover special local gifts. Stop by the Koloa History Center any day of the week from 9 a.m. to 9 p.m. to learn about the town's sweet heritage. Then cool down with an island-style Lappert's ice cream cone under the shade of the large monkey pod trees. Lappert's Ice Cream Store is a Kauai original and is still made fresh daily in nearby Hanapepe. Hawaii-inspired favorites include Heavenly Hana, Big Island Inspiration and Kauai Pie.

You can also explore the Koloa Heritage Trail, which covers 14 cultural, historical and geological sites from Old Koloa Town to Poipu. But to really experience all that this area has to offer, go to the Koloa Plantation Days Celebration (July), an annual summer event that celebrates Kauai's rich plantation past. Further south you'll discover the resorts around beautiful Poipu Beach, a modern change from charming Old Koloa Town.

Koloa Heritage Trail, Kauai

What: 10-mile tour of important sites in Koloa and Poipu

Where: South Shore of Kauai through Koloa and Poipu

Ka Ala Hele Waiwai Hooilina o Koloa, or the Koloa Heritage Trail, is a 14-stop, self-guided 10-mile tour of the Koloa and Poipu area's most important cultural, historical and geological sites, with descriptive plaques that explain each spot's significance.

Koloa is a historic South Shore area, home to Hawaii's first commercial sugar plantation. In the mid 1800's, sugar replaced the whaling industry to become the principal industry of Hawaii. As a result of the sugar boom, approximately 350,000 immigrants from around the world came to Hawaii to work in the sugar plantations. Although tourism supplanted sugar as Hawaii's major industry (Kauai's last sugar mill closed in 2008), the legacy of the era lives on in the unique ethnic diversity of Hawaii's people today.

Beyond the shower tree in the center of Old Koloa Town you'll discover the Sugar Monument, just one of the stops on the Koloa Heritage Trail. This circular concrete sculpture suggesting a millstone holds a bronze sculpture depicting the eight principal ethnic groups that brought the sugar industry to life (Hawaiian, Caucasian, Puerto Rican, Chinese, Korean, Japanese, Portuguese and Filipino). The sculpture opens up to face the remnants of the Koloa sugar mill's stone chimney, built in 1841.

Koloa Heritage Trail Locations

Encompassing the south shore of Kauai, look for these special spots on your next visit:

1. Spouting Horn Park - Famous south shore blowhole.
2. Prince Kuhio Birthplace & Park - Prince Kuhio, known as the "People's Prince," was born here in 1871.
3. Hanakaape Bay & Koloa Landing - Formerly the third largest whaling port in Hawaii.
4. Pau A Laka (Moir Gardens) - Botanical garden founded in the 1930s.
5. Kihahouna Heiau - Site of an ancient Hawaiian temple.
6. Poipu Beach Park - Popular beach home to endangered monk seals.
7. Keoneloa Bay - Home to some of Kauai's oldest occupied sites (200-600 A.D.).
8. Makaweha & Paa Dunes - A fossil bed that has become a popular spot for bird watching
9. Puuwanawana Volcanic Cone - A younger volcanic cone in a formation dating back more than 5 million years.
10. Hapa Road - Hawaiians have lived in this area since 1200 A.D.
11. Koloa Jodo Mission - Buddhist temple built in 1910.

12. Sugar Monument - Commemorates the site of Hawaii's first sugar mill.

13. Yamamoto Store & Koloa Hotel - Former plantation-era mainstay from the 1920s. Note that these two businesses are now the present day Crazy Shirts and the South Shore Pharmacy respectively.

14. Koloa Missionary Church - The first Congregational church in Kauai.

Hanalei Town

What: Charming small town on Kauai's north shore

Where: In northern Kauai, a few minutes west of Princeville

West of Princeville, on Kauai's North shore, is peaceful Hanalei Town. Graced with timeless beauty, this lovely small town is home to everything from historic places to contemporary art galleries. Hanalei Town is an unforgettable stop on your visit to Kauai.

Visit the Waioli Mission House and step back into Kauai's history. Browse Hanalei's art galleries for made-in-Kauai art and carvings made from rare, native Hawaiian woods. Locals and visitors come to Hanalei for ukulele concerts held at the Hanalei Community Center, a regular Kauai event.

At the foot of Hanalei's misty green mountains, you'll also discover fields of taro ("kalo" in Hawaiian). These heart-shaped plants grow intensely green in flooded patches and are used to make poi, a Hawaiian staple starch that you can taste at any Kauai luau. You can get a good view of this emerald quilt of land from the Hanalei Valley Lookout. Note that these taro farms are on private property, so only step foot on them during an authorized farm tour.

The historic Hanalei Pier was built in 1892 and has long been a favorite gathering place for local residents, who go there to fish, swim and play music on Hanalei Bay. In 1957, the pier became world famous when Oscar Hammerstein II and 20th Century Fox featured the pier in the classic film, "South Pacific." After a busy day of soaking up Hanalei Town's history and charm, kick back, relax and watch a luminous sunset over Hanalei Bay.

Note: To get to Hanalei, visitors need to pass over a one-lane bridge. Drivers must use local etiquette: all the vehicles on one side cross, followed by all the vehicles on the other side.

Waioli Huuia Church and Mission House

What: Hanalei landmark built in 1837

Where: In Hanalei, minutes from Princeville

Step back in time at the 1837 home of early Christian missionaries Abner and Lucy Wilcox. This Hanalei Town landmark, restored in 1921 and listed on the National Register of Historic Places, reflects the southern roots of its architect, the Reverend William Alexander of Kentucky.

Inside, synchronize your watch with the wall clock, which was installed in 1866 and still keeps perfect time. View the significant features like the lava rock chimney and the fine koa furniture. Lucy Wilcox gave birth to eight sons in the master bedroom, a significant feat on its own.

In front of the house is the old Waioli Huuia Church, which was founded in 1834. Its green shingles and stained glass windows are a picturesque symbol of Hanalei.

Tours are offered Tuesdays, Thursdays and Saturdays from 9 a.m. to 3 p.m. on a first come, first served basis.

Waioli Huuia Church and Mission House

What: Hanalei landmark built in 1837

Where: In Hanalei, minutes from Princeville

Step back in time at the 1837 home of early Christian missionaries Abner and Lucy Wilcox. This Hanalei Town landmark, restored in 1921 and listed on the National Register of Historic Places, reflects the southern roots of its architect, the Reverend William Alexander of Kentucky.

Inside, synchronize your watch with the wall clock, which was installed in 1866 and still keeps perfect time. View the significant features like the lava rock chimney and the fine koa furniture. Lucy Wilcox gave birth to eight sons in the master bedroom, a significant feat on its own.

In front of the house is the old Waioli Huuia Church, which was founded in 1834. Its green shingles and stained glass windows are a picturesque symbol of Hanalei.

Tours are offered Tuesdays, Thursdays and Saturdays from 9 a.m. to 3 p.m. on a first come, first served basis.

Grove Farm Homestead Museum

What: A historic sugar plantation museum
Where: In Lihue on Nawiliwili Road
More Info: (808) 245-3202

A visit to the Grove Farm Homestead in Lihue provides visitors with a fascinating look into the island's past. Hawaii's booming sugar plantation industry in the late 1800s had its origins on Kauai. Grove Farm, one of the earliest sugar plantations and the former home of

George N. Wilcox and his descendants, was founded in 1864. Today, this 100-acre, historic site showcases life during Kauai's plantation era more than a century ago. By appointment, a tour takes visitors throughout the property, which includes the gracious old Wilcox home and the cottage of the plantation housekeeper situated amidst tropical gardens, orchards and rolling lawns. Make a reservation and learn more about how sugar plantations influenced the history of the islands.

Note: Tours are available Monday, Wednesday, and Thursday at 10 a.m. and 1 p.m. Advanced reservations are required for the two-hour tour.

Lihue, Kauai

Lihue is the government and commercial center of the island, as well as a cultural and historical area. This may be the most traveled town on Kauai since it is home to Kauai's main airport (the Lihue Airport) and Nawiliwili Harbor, the island's major commercial shipping center and cruise ship port.

Lihue has a variety of natural wonders to explore. Kalapaki Beach is the home of the Kauai Marriott Resort and Beach Club and the Hokuala Golf Resort. Bodysurfing, SUP, surfing and swimming make

Kalapaki a popular destination. Ninini Beach is home to an automated lighthouse, in operation since 1897. And just north of Lihue, don't forget to stop at the Wailua Falls lookout for an amazing waterfall view.

The Lihue area also has numerous historical spots including Alekoko Fishpond, a roughly 1,000-year-old aquaculture reservoir; Kilohana, a historic plantation estate home to one of the island's most iconic luau; and both the historic Kauai Museum and Grove Farm Homestead Museum. Lihue is your gateway to adventure on Kauai

Kauai Museum

Name: Kauai Museum

What: Museum showcasing local artists and Hawaiian history

Where: On Rice Street in Lihue

When: Monday-Saturday 9 a.m.-4 p.m.

How Much: General admission $15, Kamaaina $10, seniors $12, students age 8-17 $10, children under 7 & active military free

More Info: (808) 245-6931

Located in a lava rock structure in Lihue, the Kauai Museum features amazing collections from the artisans of Kauai and Niihau (a small eastern island part of Kauai county). Visitors can learn about the geological formation of the Hawaiian Islands, early Native Hawaiian life, Captain Cook's arrival on Kauai's shores in Waimea and the Hawaiian Monarchy. Plus, visitors can view galleries showcasing the work of multi-cultural artists, sculptors and craftsmen. Guided tours are available (upon request).

Alekoko Fishpond

What: Legendary ancient Hawaiian fishpond
Where: In Nawiliwili, minutes from Lihue

Built nearly 1,000 years ago, the Alekoko Fishpond, minutes from Lihue, has been on the National Register of Historic Places since 1973. Ingenious ponds were built to catch fish, and this is one of the finest examples of ancient Hawaiian aquaculture.

The legend that surrounds the fishpond is based on the mythical Menehune, Hawaii's mischievous little people who performed legendary engineering feats. The Menehune lived in the forest and hid from humans. According to Hawaiian legends, the Menehune built this entire fishpond in one night. They managed this amazing task by lining up from the village of Makaweli for 25 miles, passing stones hand-to-hand to build the pond. Though Menehune legends abound, some say the word may have derived from the Tahitian word manahune meaning commoner, or small in social standing, not in physical size.

The Alekoko Fishpond is located near the Huleia National Wildlife Refuge, about a half-mile inland from Nawiliwili Harbor and can be viewed from an overlook on Hulemalu Road. The wall separating the pond from Huleia Stream is 900 feet long, five feet high and meticulously assembled with lava rock.

Note: Kayak tours are an enjoyable way to explore the fishpond. You can kayak past the pond entrance, but the refuge is closed to the public.

Napali Coast

What: Iconic, mountainous shoreline on Kauai's North Shore
Where: About 90 minutes north of Lihue

Spanning 17 miles along Kauai's North Shore, the Napali Coast is a sacred place defined by extraordinary natural beauty. These emerald-hued cliffs with razor-sharp ridges tower above the Pacific Ocean, revealing beautiful beaches and waterfalls that plummet to the lush valley floor. The rugged terrain appears much as it did centuries ago when Hawaiian settlements flourished in these deep, narrow valleys, existing only on the food they could grow and the fish they could catch.

There are many ways to explore the Napali Coast, but the safest access and best views are found by sea or by air. Boat tours depart from Port Allen on the West Side, and during the summer months, guided kayaking trips bring you up-close to soaring cathedral cliffs. When conditions are right, raft tours are available to guide you to hidden sea caves and remote beaches.

Aerial tours, most lifting off from Lihue Airport, are perhaps the best way to grasp the magnitude of the Napali Coast. You'll also get a front-row seat to scenic areas that are largely inaccessible by land or water, like majestic Manawaiopuna Falls, a backdrop in the film "Jurassic Park." Whichever tour you choose, the natural splendor of the Napali Coast will leave a deep impression on your soul.

Accommodations in Kauai

Accommodations are first in mind when tourists look for a tropical getaway. Most island resorts don't run short of accommodations for different types of guests, and Kauai is no exception. Hotels, bed and breakfasts, condos, and vacation properties are all available on the island at wide-range prices.

You have three options on where to stay on the island. You can choose to stay at the eastern shore, the tropical north shore, or the south shore. The eastern shore is also called the Coconut Coast. This is where guests will find Kapa'a and Lihu'e. Because of its central location, you will find the scenic locations of the southern shore or the taro fields of the north all within easy reach. The town is also near the island airport, with various accommodations in the form of hotels, condos, and apartments, all dotting the coastline.

The north shore is famous for its luxurious resorts. This is where you can get a glimpse of the famous Na Pali Coast and stay in one of the luxury resorts of Princeville and Hanalei, which come with tennis courts, golf courses, and fine dining restaurants. You can also head to Poipu, where guests can stay at one of the tropical plantation cottages for rent. Poipu Beach has been named as one of America's best beaches by beach experts.

Kauai hotels

Kauai hotels are often the first option for first-time holiday-goers because of its many benefits. For one, guests can expect transportation service from the airport, daily maid service, and the full use of resort amenities. Kauai hotels are the perfect place for those who plan on staying for a short period of time. You can enjoy relaxing hours at the spa and enjoy full luxury in units that feature hardwood floors, Jacuzzis, lavish decor, four-poster beds, and complete amenities.

A few of the top hotels in Kauai include the Grand Hyatt Kauai Resort and Spa and Kauai Marriot Resort & Beach Club. The Kauai Marriot features lush tropical palm trees that stand over a blue swimming pool that overlooks the Kalapaki Beach and features 51 acres of lush tropical gardens. Another prime luxury hotel is Sheraton Kauai Resort, surrounded by one of the island's premiere beaches.

For cheaper accommodations, you can check in to the Kalaheo Inn, with easy reach to the island's popular hiking and trekking destinations.

Kauai condos

Condos are the perfect accommodation option for those who plan on staying in the island for longer than a short vacation period. Guests have the option of choosing small, cozy units, or large, sprawling estates, perfect for large families and definitely more cost-effective than renting multiple hotel rooms. For those looking for condominium accommodations, the Kauai Resorts are also a good perfect option. Just a few steps from the beaches of Kauai, some resort in this island boasts of studios and bedroom accommodations styled in the latest architectural designs. Guests are also treated to calming garden and oceanfront views.

Renting a condo also allows guests more flexibility in hours and lengths of stay, unlike timeshares where guests are locked into specific check-in and check-out dates. However, some tourists may also stay away from condos because they are definitely more expensive than timeshare units and may also come with cleaning fees added to the rent. Cleaning fees are usually collected on a two-week basis, and for most condos, guests are expected to pay cleaning fees worth two weeks even if they are booked to stay for only a few days. To top it all off, condos do not have some of the amenities that guests look for in a hotel.

Kauai timeshare units

Kauai timeshare resorts allow guests to exchange into a resort in Kauai, made available by private owners and by management companies. Expert holiday-goers will tell you that renting a timeshare unit is one of the best ways to spend your days in Kauai. There are various sizes of timeshares to choose from, from two bedroom units to units that can accommodate up to six people. There is no cleaning fee for most timeshare units, but guests can expect to pay timeshare taxes for each week, depending on the size of the unit.

Curious holiday-goers can rent lodgings from owners' villas, apartments, homes, and cottages by searching for matches online.

Bed and breakfasts

Although not as popular as the other three, bed and breakfasts also enjoy the reputation as one of the least expensive ways to stay on the island. Bed and breakfasts in the island include the Aloha Plantation Bread and Breakfast, Hale Luana Bed and Breakfast, and the River Estate Guest House. Bed and breakfasts are cozy, traditional, and come with home cooked meals and the quaint, homey comforts not seen in plush hotels. Bed and breakfasts are also the perfect option for those who want to stay in a place of history, such as plantation era homes, and for those who prefer the quiet seclusion compared to the more crowded commercial establishments on the island.

Hostels

For students and those looking for a rugged holiday in the tropics, hostels are the perfect option, ranging from locations with four to six units each, some with shared baths. Prices range from $25 to $55 for each room, depending on the type of accommodation. You also have the option of camping with hostels that have available camping grounds and tents for rent. Some hostels allow children under five years old to stay for free.

There are quite a lot of options for accommodations in the island. For a quick run-through on the most popular cottages, resorts, condos, and villas, here's a shortlist:

Kauai Cove Cottages

This is a nice and quaint resort in Poipu that is known for being secluded and for being one of the best places for a honeymoon, or at best, a secluded getaway. The place features a tropical Hawaiian decor with a twin canopy bed, a private patio, and a full kitchen for each cottage. It also enjoys a prime spot between Poipu Beach and Shipwreck Beach.

Ka Hale O Luina

This is another establishment that offers the best in tropical island comfort. Located near Poipu, the Ka Hale O Luina is known for its classic fusion of Bali architecture and the modern island lifestyle. This is the perfect getaway for those who are looking for seclusion and romance with all the comforts of a luxury spa.

Bamboo Jungle House

The Bamboo Jungle House sits on the south side of the island where it benefits from prevailing trade winds. Guests like you are treated to panoramic views of the ocean and the island's majestic mountains. The place is within easy reach from the Old Koloa Town. Those who love the ocean will enjoy the waters and pristine sands of Poipu Beach, known as one of the best beaches in the world. The place is only a short distance away from the Lihue Airport.

Aloha Kauai Villas

Located just a few miles from the Polihale Beach, the villas provide a place of relaxation amidst lush tropical vegetation. Each villa contains three or four bedrooms, all of which are beautifully furnished. Each villa has something that makes it unique. Villa I overlooks a hot spa and has a majestic view of the Pacific Ocean, while Villa II features a hot tub. Villa III is just a few steps from the water.

Outrigger At Lae Nani

This resort is perfect for golfers because of its championship golf course and relaxing oceanfront vistas. The resort is located on the island's eastern shore with spacious one- and two-bedroom units, which come with the latest amenities. The resort also has an oceanfront swimming pool and tennis courts.

Banyan Harbor Resort

Guests can choose to stay in one of the many well appointed units, which have their own separate living rooms, dining rooms, and bedrooms. These units are equipped with bath and showers, television sets, and full-sized kitchens, as well as dishwashers, ovens, cable TVs, air conditioning, and large bath tubs.

Garden Island Properties

Garden island Properties features a number of quaint vacation rentals, real estates, and prime honeymoon spots scattered all over the island, with their own unique view of the coastline and Kauai's beaches. You can go rustic with a small cottage on the beach, or enjoy a slice of modern island life with a well appointed condo that comes with a whirlpool Jacuzzi and tub. Garden Island Properties also handles the selling or buying of real estate in the island.

Kauai Sands Hotel

Finally, the Kauai Sands Hotel is the perfect place for families, honeymooners, and groups of friends alike. Newly redone in contemporary architecture, Kauai Sands Hotel also has Internet access, a beachfront pool, and other services. Those looking for exercise in-between relaxing lounges by the pool can play tennis or golf at the resort's tennis courts and golf courses.

With a long list of accommodation options, almost any type of traveler is welcome to stay in the island of Kauai. To make the most of your vacation or travel adventure, it would be best to make reservations weeks in advance or at least make a list of possible choices that meet your budget requirements and personal preferences.

Aston Islander on the Beach

Located on the east coast of Kauai Island, the Aston Islander on the Beach (formerly Resortquest) is a low-rise, plantation-style hotel with eight three-story buildings with 198 guest rooms. Refurbished in 2005, the hotel boasts of superb ocean and garden views for each room.

From Lihue airport, exit from Ahukini Road to get to the hotel. Make a right at Kapule Higway 51; the street name will change to Kuhio Highway 56. Watch out for Aston Islander on the Beach on your right, adjacent to the Coconut Plantation Marketplace.

Room rates and amenities

Hotel rooms at Aston Islander on the Beach have rates that range from $214 to $306 a night, while one-bedroom suites cost $332 a night. There are also eSpecial rates for the Aston Islander, which are exclusively for guests who will book online. For standard hotel rooms, the eSpecial rate ranges from $137 to 208 per night, and $268 for one-bedroom suites per night. Rates may vary according to the season.

There are four kinds of guestrooms at the Aston Islander: The Garden View room, located on the ground floor, which has one king bed or two double beds, a sofa bed, and lanai with view of the gardens; Ocean Front room, located closest to the ocean, which has one king bed or two double beds, a sofa bed, and lanai with panoramic Pacific view; Ocean View room, with one king bed or two double beds a sofa bed and lanai with full Pacific view; and Partial Ocean View room, which is located on the top floor, with one king bed or two double beds, a sofa bed, and lanai with partial ocean view.

All rooms have the following amenities: Internet access, cable/satellite flat screenTV, coffee/tea maker, complimentary toiletries, air conditioning, CD and cassette player, balcony, patio, refrigerator, hair dryer, clock radio, iron/ironing board, voice mail, complimentary newspaper, cribs (infant beds), microwave, shower/tub combination and in-room safe.

Aston Islander on the Beach also follows Hawaii's Non-Smoking Law -- all accommodations in the hotel do not allow smoking.

Services

A public swimming pool and spa tub is set up at the hotel, as well as barbecue grills and a picnic area. Guests bringing cars automatically have free parking. Wireless Internet access is also available, as well as laundry facilities and babysitting/child care services. Pets are not allowed in Aston Islander.

Activities

The hotel is located just a half mile from the beach where guests can do a variety of activities. They can go snorkeling or surfing, play volleyball, or relax on the sand. The resort also has its own pool and spa tub.

Other features

Although Aston Islander does not have an in-house restaurant, the Coconut Plantation Marketplace is just a short walk away. It houses over 60 specialty shops and restaurants.

There is also the Wailua Golf Course, which is also a short walk from the hotel. Those interested to go boating or kayaking can visit the Wailua River, which is the longest navigable river in Hawaii.

Aston Islander on the Beach is at 440 Aleka Place, Kapaa, Kauai, Hawaii. Its magnificent ocean view is perfect for any island getaway

Aston at Poipu Kai Formerly Resort Quest

Aston at Poipu Kai, which was formerly known as ResortQuest, is a plantation-style 315-room condominium resort that occupies 70 acres in South Kauai, Hawaii. It is strategically placed because you can easily walk along a half-mile path to the world-class Shipwreck Beach and

Poipu Beach. Shipwreck Beach is ideal for surfing or simply beach walking. A man-made reef had been constructed to protect the lower loop of the S-shaped Poipu Beach so that the water is calm. Meanwhile, you can snorkel among the lava rocks that are located around a sand inlet. This part of Poipu Beach can also be used for boogie boarding or surfing. The property also has the benefit of being only 10.5 miles away from the Lihue Airport.

Condominium resort amenities

One of the key features of Aston at Poipu Kai are the six swimming pools that are found throughout the resort, including two hot tubs. Each pool has a barbecue grill that you may use. Other convenient features include the following: tour assistance; provision of picnic areas; concierge services; Internet access in the lobby and in other public areas; various business services; babysitting services; free parking; free reading of newspapers in the lobby; rental of videotapes; putting green; tennis courts; jet spas; and a scenic trail that is ideal for walking or jogging; and a safe-deposit box that is available at the front desk.

Room amenities and characteristics

All rooms are non-smoking and are provided with patios and lanais that offer views of the hotel's tropical grounds. While there are differences in room decoration, most of them have Hawaiian print fabrics and rattan furniture. Ceiling fans are provided instead of air-conditioners to maintain the tropical ambiance but there are many windows for adequate ventilation.

The rooms are provided with fully equipped kitchens and have satellite or cable television. Other room features include housekeeping services, hair dryer, coffee maker, microwave oven, clock radio, CD player, free local telephone calls, cribs when needed, VCR, voice mail, refrigerator, in-room safe, and ironing board.

Where to go for food

If you prefer a casual dining experience, you can head to Brennecke's Beach Broiler at Hoone Road, which is well-known for its fish dinners that you can enjoy along with sunset views. Along the Kuhio Highway, you can also enjoy inexpensive family-style cooking at the Kountry Kitchen for lunch or breakfast. For some beer and fun food, you can go to the Waimea Brewing Co., which is found along the Kaumualii Highway at the Aston Waimea Plantation Cottages.

For fine dining, you may go to The Bull Shed, which is located along the Kuhio Highway, for some steaks and other high-quality food. Another place to go is the Bali Hai restaurant at the Hanalei Bay Resort in Princeville for some Pacific-Rim cooking. You may also enjoy this kind of food at Gaylord's at Kilohana along the Kaumualii Highway.

For fast food service, you may want to try Duane's Ono Char, which sells hamburgers along the Kuhio Highway. You may also go to the Aloha Kauai Pizza, which is also located along the Kuhio Highway, for some pizza and other kinds of Italian cooking.

Aston Waimea Plantation Cottages

The Aston Waimea Plantation Cottages, which were formerly known as ResortQuest, occupy an area of 27 acres. The cottages are nestled inside a peaceful coconut grove and provide you with an insight into the past of Hawaii, particularly as a group of sugar plantation islands. This plantation-style resort that is made up of real cottages is found on the western coast of Kauai Island that are equipped with furniture that try to mimic those employed during that period of Hawaii's past. These cottages had been occupied by the workers of the Waimea Sugar Mill Co.

This resort provides a natural setting for the cottages so that you really feel you are vacationing in the tropics. There are beautiful gardens and very tall coconut trees that could have existed during that period when the area was a plantation of the sugar company. The beach front of this property has a good-size swimming pool with a matching huge sunning deck that also has a hot tub.

Hotel features

This particular Aston resort is primarily suited for exploring both South Kauai and West Kauai because it is found in a thinly populated non-resort area in Waimea. Other important characteristics include a poolside bar; barbecue grills; spa services; picnic area; hair salon; gift shops; health club; newsstand; free parking; video library; gardens; free reading of newspapers at the lobby; free Internet access in public areas; wireless access to the Internet in the rooms; and laundry facilities.

Possible recreational activities

Some of the possible recreational activities within the area include golfing, parasailing, volleyball, skydiving, hiking, biking, boating, horse riding, snorkeling, and fishing. Personal watercraft can be rented and you can also go rafting, boogie boarding, surfing, and helicopter sightseeing.

Room features

There are 56 cottages available for guests in the plantation. The cottages have been restored to imitate the decorations and design employed in the 1930s and 1940s. Every cottage is provided with furniture made from rattan, wicker and mahogany. All rooms are non-smoking, and have upholstered seatings and wooden floors. However, they are provided with the modern conveniences of a bathroom, such as bathtubs, pedestal sinks, and spacious and separate shower stalls. Dial-up Internet access may also be available if requested in advance.

Other room features include cable or satellite television, coffee maker, clock radio, telephone, ceiling fan, CD player, hair dryer, ironing board and iron, VCR, crib when requested, voice mail, cooking facilities, dry cleaning services, and in-room safe.

Where to go for food

When you get hungry after all the fun and leisure, you may visit the Waimea Brewing Company that offers various kinds of ethnic food and handcrafted beer. Other places to go include the Shrimp Station along the Kaumualii Highway in Waimea; the Ishihara Market, which is a delicatessen that is also found along the Kaumualii Highway in Waimea; Wrangler's Steakhouse, which serves Polynesian food, seafood items, and steaks, also along the Kaumualii Highway, Waimea; Obsessions Cafe along Waimea Road in Waimea; and the Kokee Lodge Restaurant, which serves continental food at Kokee Road, Waimea.

Castle Kaha Lani, A Condominium Resort

Castle Kaha Lani Resort in Lihue in the Hawaiian island of Kauai is only two miles from the Coconut Marketplace of Kauai and only a quarter of a mile to the south of the Royal Coconut Coast. Its 35 resort rooms are actually condominium suites that are all facing the ocean to provide you with a beautiful view of the ocean, tropical gardens, and white sandy beaches. The resort is conveniently located because it is only five miles from the Lihue Airport.

The comforts of home

The resort rooms are all individually furnished to provide you with the feeling that you are home but with the added advantage of having the Pacific Ocean right there in your front yard. Every room has its own lanai that provide you with views of landscaped lawns, tropical gardens, and the ocean. Each room has cable television and completely equipped kitchens. Most important of all is that your room is only yards away from the sandy beaches.

Resort amenities for your convenience and pleasure

The resort has swimming pools with heaters to make sure that the water temperature is just right. Other features of this condominium resort are a putting green, tennis court, sun deck, barbecue area, a coin-operated laundromat, wireless Internet access, and complimentary parking.

Non-smoking rooms are available for those who prefer them. The kitchens are all provided with coffee makers, toasters, dishwashers, and microwave ovens. Every room has cable television and some rooms even have VCRs. Other conveniences of the rooms include a private lanai that is provided with chairs and tables, shower, bathtub, telephone, hair dryer, a clock, radio, and ceiling fan. Some of the rooms even have their own safes for locking away your valuables.

A room with one bedroom has a queen-size bed, one bathroom, and has more than 600 square feet of living space, excluding the lanai that has an area of 150 square feet. A room with two bedrooms and two bathrooms has a queen-size bed, a sofa bed, and two twins. Its living space is more than 900 square feet and its lanai may have a space of 246 square feet. A three-bedroom suite has two bathrooms, two queen-size beds, a sofa bed, and two twins. Its living space is more than 1,100 square feet and the area of its lanai is 253 square feet.

Sports and recreation

You may want to engage in various beach activities including snorkeling. You can also practice your golf at the resort's putting greens or you can play a whole round of golf at a nearby course. You can practice your tennis swings at the resort's tennis courts. For those who love to swim, the swimming pool is only yards away.

Possible activities at Kauai

The Poipu Bay Golf Course is where the PGA Grand Slam of Golf is held. You can play golf in unique landscapes with lava tubes, streams, and waterfalls. You may also try kayaking or windsurfing. Or you can paddle your boat along the Wailua River. You can also go diving or snorkeling at the Makua Beach on the North Shore.

Castle Kiahuna Plantation & Beach Bungalows

Indulge yourself in lush, tropical surroundings at the Castle Kiahuna Plantation and Beach Bungalows. This Hawaiian paradise spans 35 landscaped acres filled gardens, ornamental ponds, and the ocean. It combines the 19th century Hawaiian sugar plantation era with all the modern amenities -- perfect for a peaceful getaway for any occasion.

Room rates and amenities

Castle Kiahuna Plantation and Beach Bungalows houses condominium-type units. Guests can choose from one-bedroom/one-bathroom or two-bedroom/two-bathroom rooms, or they can go for all-out luxury with the beachfront suites. The two-bed/two-bath suites are all split-level and furnished with a fully-equipped kitchen.

Choose your room based on the view you want to enjoy during your stay. Garden View rooms (Deluxe or Paradise) surround guests with an array of tropical fruits, flowers, cacti, plumeria trees, hibiscus shrubs, and bougainvillea vines. Partial Ocean View rooms are just a few steps from the beach, while Ocean View rooms give guests a beautiful view of the blue horizon. At the Beachfront Alii Suite, expect nothing less than white sand to greet you at your doorway, and high-quality and unique furnishings to give each guest a different experience.

Each room is equipped with the following amenities: private lanai with table and chairs; full kitchen equipped with microwave, dish washer, coffee maker and blender; electronic key card; ceiling fan; in-room safe; hair dryer; shower/tub; iron/ironing board; clock/radio; color cable TV; and two-line phone with data port. Ocean View and Beachfront units have upgraded amenities such as enhanced maid service, daily newspaper and Kauai coffee, and robe and slippers. Non-smoking units are available.

Services

Complimentary parking is available to all guests at Castle Kiahuna Plantation and Beach Bungalows. High-speed Internet access for traveling businessmen is also available. Long-staying guests can do their laundry at the coin-operated laundromat. Babysitting can also be arranged for families, and couples who want to have their wedding at the resort can be referred to a wedding planner.

For dining options, guests can visit the Plantation Garden Restaurant within the resort, which is open for dinner and cocktails. The Poipu Beach area is also littered with many dining establishments.

Activities

Being situated near the beach means guests will never run out of activities at Castle Kiahuna Plantation and Beach Bungalows. Guests can go sailing, surfing, fishing or kayaking, or even request a helicopter tour of the island.

Barbecue areas are also situated throughout the resort. A "Super Pool" with a water slide is also at the resort, as well as four tennis courts for sports buffs to enjoy. A three-minute drive from the resort brings guests to the Kiahuna Golf Course, and ten minutes away is the famous Poipu Bay Resort Golf Course.

Other features

Half a mile away from the resort are the Moir gardens, which are filled with shaped cacti, 70-year-old orchids, ancient Hawaiian lava-rock walls, and artifacts like a grinding stone from Hawaii's first sugar mill, and a whaler's melting pot converted into a water-lily planter.

Guests can also visit sites like the Kauai Coffee Company, Hawaii's largest coffee plantation, the Waimea Canyon, and the Sprouting Horn, where surf and lava meet.

Be it for your family, a honeymoon, or a business trip, set your vacation at the Castle Kiahuna Plantation and Beach Bungalows to treat yourself to a tropical paradise that blends old Hawaii perfectly with the new.

Castle Lae Nani, A Condominium Resort

Castle Lae Nani is an ocean front condominium resort set amid tropical gardens that lead to the beach on Wailua Bay. There are 80 available suites in a three-story building located along the Papaloa Road in Kapaa in the island of Kauai in Hawaii. This luxury resort is only 10 minutes away from the Lihue Airport and various shops, restaurants, and activities can be reached by foot.

Property features

The Castle Lae Nani luxury resort offers condominium suites with either one bedroom or two bedrooms, lanais for viewing the Pacific Ocean, and fully equipped kitchens. Housekeeping services are available for stays that are at least seven days long.

Important features of the condominium resort include an outdoor swimming pool, picnic area, barbecue grills, free parking, laundry facilities, business services, patio, and sun deck.

Activities for recreation and sports include golf, swimming, snorkeling, sailing, kayaking, diving, and other kinds of water sports. Swimming is possible both in the pool or in the beach.

Room features

All condominium suites are non-smoking and are provided with a lanai with chairs and a table for your comfortable viewing of the beautiful ocean. The kitchen is provided with a coffee maker, blender, and microwave oven. Other room features include a washer and dryer for some units, ceiling fan, telephone, videocassette recorder, clock radio, color television, wet bar, shower and tub, and hair dryer.

Where to go to eat

When you get hungry after all those activities, you may walk to the Coconut Marketplace, which has more than 70 eateries and shops. Other restaurants are also available in Kapaa, including Hukilau Lanai for Hawaiian cuisine; the Kauai Pasta Kapaa for Italian food; the Kountry Kitchen for breakfast and brunch only for American cuisine; Mermaids Cafe; Pho Vy for Vietnamese cuisine; Verde Restaurant for

Mexican food; Scotty's Beachside Barbeque; the Ono Family Restaurant for eclectic and American cuisine; and Wahoo's Seafood Grill and Bar.

Possible activities in Kapaa

A very popular activity in Kapaa is the Steelgrass Farm Chocolate Farm Tour, where participants are given the chance to taste the different varieties of chocolate and listen to a lecture on various chocolate facts. Other activities include the Kayak Wailua tour, a visit to the Kauai Aadheenam Hindu Monastery, a round of golf at the Wailua Golf Course, participation in Deep Sea Fishing Kauai, Coconut Coasters Beach Bike Rentals, treetop ziplining through the assistance of the company Just Live, Hawaii Movie Tours of the places where Raiders of the Lost Ark and Jurassic Park were filmed, a visit to the Kahn Galleries, and some drinks at the Kauai Tradewinds bar and club.

For some horseback riding, you can go to the Esprit De Corps Riding Academy. You can also join a group tour by boat in the Snuba Tours of Kauai. If you enjoy hiking, you may want to follow the Sleeping Giant Trail, which is located along the Nounou Road. Other well-known attractions in Kapaa include the Kamalani Playground, Kealia Beach, Kinipopo Fine Art, Wyland Gallery, Donkey Beach, and Birds in Paradise.

Castle Kiahuna Plantation & Beach Bungalows

Indulge your self in lush, tropical surroundings at the Castle Kiahuna Plantation and Beach Bungalows. This Hawaiian paradise spans 35 landscaped acres filled gardens, ornamental ponds, and the ocean. It combines the 19th century Hawaiian sugar plantation era with all the modern amenities -- perfect for a peaceful getaway for any occasion.

Room rates and amenities

Castle Kiahuna Plantation and Beach Bungalows houses condominium-type units. Guests can choose from one-bedroom/one-bathroom or two-bedroom/two-bathroom rooms, or they can go for all-out luxury with the beachfront suites. The two-bed/two-bath suites are all split-level and furnished with a fully-equipped kitchen.

Choose your room based on the view you want to enjoy during your stay. Garden View rooms (Deluxe or Paradise) surround guests with an array of tropical fruits, flowers, cacti, plumeria trees, hibiscus shrubs, and bougainvillea vines. Partial Ocean View rooms are just a few steps from the beach, while Ocean View rooms give guests a beautiful view of the blue horizon. At the Beachfront Alii Suite, expect nothing less than white sand to greet you at your doorway, and high-quality and unique furnishings to give each guest a different experience.

Each room is equipped with the following amenities: private lanai with table and chairs; full kitchen equipped with microwave, dish washer, coffee maker and blender; electronic key card; ceiling fan; in-room safe; hair dryer; shower/tub; iron/ironing board; clock/radio; color cable TV; and two-line phone with data port. Ocean View and Beachfront units have upgraded amenities such as enhanced maid service, daily newspaper and Kauai coffee, and robe and slippers. Non-smoking units are available.

Services

Complimentary parking is available to all guests at Castle Kiahuna Plantation and Beach Bungalows. High-speed Internet access for traveling businessmen is also available. Long-staying guests can do their laundry at the coin-operated laundromat. Babysitting can also be arranged for families, and couples who want to have their wedding at the resort can be referred to a wedding planner.

For dining options, guests can visit the Plantation Garden Restaurant within the resort, which is open for dinner and cocktails. The Poipu Beach area is also littered with many dining establishments.

Activities

Being situated near the beach means guests will never run out of activities at Castle Kiahuna Plantation and Beach Bungalows. Guests can go sailing, surfing, fishing or kayaking, or even request a helicopter tour of the island.

Barbecue areas are also situated throughout the resort. A "Super Pool" with a water slide is also at the resort, as well as four tennis courts for sports buffs to enjoy. A three-minute drive from the resort brings guests to the Kiahuna Golf Course, and ten minutes away is the famous Poipu Bay Resort Golf Course.

Other features

Half a mile away from the resort are the Moir gardens, which are filled with shaped cacti, 70-year-old orchids, ancient Hawaiian lava-rock walls, and artifacts like a grinding stone from Hawaii's first sugar mill, and a whaler's melting pot converted into a water-lily planter.

Guests can also visit sites like the Kauai Coffee Company, Hawaii's largest coffee plantation, the Waimea Canyon, and the Sprouting Horn, where surf and lava meet.

Be it for your family, a honeymoon, or a business trip, set your vacation at the Castle Kiahuna Plantation and Beach Bungalows to treat yourself to a tropical paradise that blends old Hawaii perfectly with the new.

Castle Lae Nani, A Condominium Resort

Castle Lae Nani is an ocean front condominium resort set amid tropical gardens that lead to the beach on Wailua Bay. There are 80 available suites in a three-story building located along the Papaloa Road in Kapaa in the island of Kauai in Hawaii. This luxury resort is only 10 minutes away from the Lihue Airport and various shops, restaurants, and activities can be reached by foot.

Property features

The Castle Lae Nani luxury resort offers condominium suites with either one bedroom or two bedrooms, lanais for viewing the Pacific Ocean, and fully equipped kitchens. Housekeeping services are available for stays that are at least seven days long.

Important features of the condominium resort include an outdoor swimming pool, picnic area, barbecue grills, free parking, laundry facilities, business services, patio, and sun deck.

Activities for recreation and sports include golf, swimming, snorkeling, sailing, kayaking, diving, and other kinds of water sports. Swimming is possible both in the pool or in the beach.

Room features

All condominium suites are non-smoking and are provided with a lanai with chairs and a table for your comfortable viewing of the beautiful ocean. The kitchen is provided with a coffee maker, blender, and microwave oven. Other room features include a washer and dryer for some units, ceiling fan, telephone, videocassette recorder, clock radio, color television, wet bar, shower and tub, and hair dryer.

Where to go to eat

When you get hungry after all those activities, you may walk to the Coconut Marketplace, which has more than 70 eateries and shops. Other restaurants are also available in Kapaa, including Hukilau Lanai for Hawaiian cuisine; the Kauai Pasta Kapaa for Italian food; the Kountry Kitchen for breakfast and brunch only for American cuisine; Mermaids Cafe; Pho Vy for Vietnamese cuisine; Verde Restaurant for Mexican food; Scotty's Beachside Barbeque; the Ono Family Restaurant for eclectic and American cuisine; and Wahoo's Seafood Grill and Bar.

Possible activities in Kapaa

A very popular activity in Kapaa is the Steelgrass Farm Chocolate Farm Tour, where participants are given the chance to taste the different varieties of chocolate and listen to a lecture on various chocolate facts. Other activities include the Kayak Wailua tour, a visit to the Kauai Aadheenam Hindu Monastery, a round of golf at the Wailua Golf Course, participation in Deep Sea Fishing Kauai, Coconut Coasters Beach Bike Rentals, treetop ziplining through the assistance of the company Just Live, Hawaii Movie Tours of the places where Raiders of the Lost Ark and Jurassic Park were filmed, a visit to the Kahn Galleries, and some drinks at the Kauai Tradewinds bar and club.

For some horseback riding, you can go to the Esprit De Corps Riding Academy. You can also join a group tour by boat in the Snuba Tours of Kauai. If you enjoy hiking, you may want to follow the Sleeping Giant Trail, which is located along the Nounou Road. Other well-known attractions in Kapaa include the Kamalani Playground, Kealia Beach, Kinipopo Fine Art, Wyland Gallery, Donkey Beach, and Birds in Paradise.

Castle Lanikai, A Condominium Resort

The Castle Lanikai is a condominium resort that is located along the Papaloa Road in Kapaa in the island of Kauai in Hawaii. This property is found on the southern end of the popular Royal Coconut Coast and it is only five and a half miles from the Lihue Airport. This resort is only yards away to the Wailua Beach. The Coconut Coast is a strip of beaches that is eight miles long with beautiful views of the ocean.

Property features

The primary feature of this condominium resort is the peaceful environment with its rich tropical gardens, manicured lawns, and breathtaking ocean views. There are only 18 available suites that are found in two buildings that are three stories high. There are no elevators and access to the upper floors is through external staircases.

There is an outdoor swimming pool with barbecue grills and a picnic area. There are free newspapers in the lobby and parking is also free. Recreational activities within the area include golfing, boogie boarding, snorkeling, tennis, surfing, parasailing, volleyball, skydiving, boating, hiking, biking, sightseeing through helicopter or airplane, horseback riding, fishing, sailing, enjoyment of personal watercraft, rafting, and kayaking.

Room features

The wide balconies and patios of the Castle Lanikai, A Condominium Resort, offer you with ocean views. Island-style decoration is employed in the rooms that have fully equipped kitchens, washers, and dryers. Other room features include a clock radio, microwave oven, hair dryer, coffee maker, free local telephone calls, satellite and cable television, videocassette recorder, cookware, utensils, dishes, refrigerator, iron board, iron, crib when requested, and ceiling fan.

Where to go to eat

While the Castle Lanikai, A Condominium Resort, does not have its own restaurant, there are different dining places within the area. These include the Bali Hai Restaurant at Princeville for some fine dining; Brennecke's Beach Broiler at Hoone Road in Poipu Beach, Koloa, for some casual dining right there on the beach; A Pacific Cafe restaurant at the Kauai Village in Kapaa that is owned by Jean-Marie Josselin; and Duke's Canoe Club restaurant at Rice Street on Kalapaki Beach, for dining with Hawaiian music.

Other places to go for dining include Chuck's Steak House at the Princeville Shopping Center for salads, fresh fish, desserts, and wine; Wind's of Beamreach Restaurant at Princeville for American cuisine including steaks, seafood and pasta; Hale O' Java restaurant at the Princeville Shopping Center for gourmet pizza, pasta, homemade pastries, and gourmet coffee; and the Gaylord's at Kilohana restaurant at the Kilohana Plantation Estate along Kaumualii Highway, Lihue for international cuisine in a plantation setting.

Still more dining places are the Hanalei Taro and Juice Co. for original taro products; The Bull Shed restaurant along Kuhio Highway in Kapaa; Keoki's Paradise restaurant at the Kiahuna Shopping Center, Kiahuna Plantation Drive in Koloa, for prime steaks, seafood, and fresh fish; the Kahanu Snack Bar at the Aloha Beach Resort Kauai; the Restaurant Kintaro Japanese Steak House at Kuhio Highway in Kapaa; and the House of Seafood along Poipu Road.

Castle Makahuena, A Condominium Resort At Poipu

Head to Kauai island's southernmost tip and there you'll find luxury like no other - at Castle Makahuena.

Situated at the famous Poipu beach, the condo-resort lets guests enjoy full sunrise and sunset views. Seventy-nine condominium units house two- and three-story, plantation-style wood buildings, all individually furnished with a distinct look.

Room rates and amenities

Guests can choose among one- ($270-$325), two- ($300-$520), or three-bedroom ($380-475) suites, along with the view they want. Garden View rooms overlook Makahuena's tropical gardens, filled with hibiscus, bougainvillea and other exotic plant life. For an unobstructed view of the Pacific, guests can opt for ocean front suites.

Stairs provided access to rooms on upper floors, as there are no elevators in this resort. All rooms are equipped with ceiling fans and high-speed Internet access.

Other amenities include the following: coffee/tea maker, hair dryer, balcony, cribs (upon request), free local calls, clock radio, in-room safe, iron/ironing board, kitchen, microwave, cookware/dishes/utensils and refrigerator. For guests staying longer than seven days, housekeeping services are provided for free. Children who are 17 years old and younger can stay for free, with existing bedding. Additional beds may be requested at an extra charge.

Services

Parking is complimentary for all guests here at Castle Makahuena. Babysitting services may be requested when needed. A whirlpool/hot tub is readily available for guests looking for rest and relaxation. A safe deposit box is available at the front desk. Pets are not allowed in Castle Makahuena.

Activities and other features

The resort has its own pool, tennis courts, and barbecue area, but guests at Castle Makahuena are within easy access to different activity-filled areas in Kauai. Closest is Poipu Beach, where the waters are gentle enough for snorkeling. Also nearby are Mahaulepu and Shipwreck beaches, where whale-watching, sailing, kayaking, fishing, parasailing and surfing/boogie boarding are just some of the favorite activities.

Guests can appreciate more the nearly unspoiled beauty of Kauai by going through laid out hiking trails or by renting a helicopter for a bird's eye view tour of the island. Horseback riding can be enjoyed by the kids, while the more adventurous can go mountain biking. Golf enthusiasts can trek to the nearby Poipu Bay Golf Course or the Kiahuna Golf Course.

Although the resort does not have its own restaurant, guests will never run out of food choices in the surrounding area. There's the Plantations Garden Restaurant, Roy's Poipu Bar and Grill, Beach House Restaurant, Shell's Steak and Seafood, and Keoki's Paradise, to name a few.

The Lihue Airport is the closest one to Castle Makahuena, and it is approximately 15 miles or 30 minutes away. After exiting Lihue Airport, continue straight ahead from the first intersection on Ahukini

Road. Make a left at Kuhio Highway / Highway 56, and stay on the right lane until it merges with Kaumualii Highway West / Highway 50. Turn left at Maluhia Road / Highway 520 amd follow it for two miles. Make a left when you see Ala Kinoiki Highway on your left (which is also the first intersection). Follow the highway until you reach the Poipu Road intersection. Drive across Poipu Road which turns into Pe'e Road. Castle Makahuena at Poipu is located on the left side of the road, just past The Point at Poipu resort. Castle Makahuena is at 1661 Pe`e Road.

Wyndham Bali Hai Villas

Wyndham Bali Hai Villas is part of Wyndham Vacation Resorts and is found in the Pepelani Loop in Princeville, Kauai, Hawaii. The 85-room resort is located high in the cliff terrain of Princeville to provide you with magnificent views of the North Shore of Kauai and the mountains that span the whole Hanalei Valley. Important to golf enthusiasts is the fact that it is sandwiched by two world-class golf courses, which are the Princeville Golf Club-Makai Course and the Princeville Golf Club-Prince Course. It is also only 30 miles away from the Lihue Airport.

Property features

The resort boasts of outdoor swimming pools, including a pool designed for children and a hot tub. Other amenities include a picnic or barbecue area, a clubhouse, a tennis court, and accessible units. Other services include Internet access, laundry facilities, free Internet access when you are in the public areas, free parking, and tour assistance. Possible activities in the area include playing around in the sandy beaches, fishing, relaxing in a day spa, windsurfing, boating, shopping, golf, hiking, scuba diving, snorkeling, horseback riding, and enjoying some live entertainment.

Room features

The furnishings of the rooms include desks and sofa beds. The one-bedroom accommodation has one king size bed and one queen size bed, while the two-bedroom accommodation has one king size bed and two double beds. Room conveniences include wireless Internet access, pay movies, DVD player, premium television channels, premium bedding, air conditioning, climate control, ceiling fan, distinct sitting area, coffee maker, microwave oven, fully-equipped kitchen, refrigerator, shower and tub, private bathroom, housekeeping services, clock radio, sofa bed, desk, hair dryer, roll-away beds, crib when requested, washer and dryer, cookware, ironing board and iron, and electronic keys.

Where to go to eat

There are two notable restaurants within Princeville, Kauai. One is the Italian restaurant known as Sabelle's At Princeville LLC along Ka Haku Road. The other place to eat in Princeville is the Prince Restaurant & Bar along Kuhio Highway. Other important restaurants within the area include the Sushi Blues Japanese restaurant at Hanalei along Kuhio Highway; The Living Room in Princeville along Ka Haku Road; and The Beach Restaurant at Princeville along Ka Haku Road.

For casual dining, the places to go within the Princeville area are all in Hanalei. These include the Polynesian Cafe in the Ching Young Village Shops; Bourbon Street Cafe at the Kuhio Highway; Subway also at the Kuhio Highway; The Hanalei Gourmet, again at the Kuhio Highway; and Pizza Hanalei at the Ching Young Village Shops. For seafood, you may want to try The Winds of Beamreach Restaurant at Hanalei along Ka Haku Road. For steaks, you can try Chuck's Steak House also at Hanalei at the Princeville Center.

Attractions within the Princeville area

You may want to visit the Kaua'i Children's Discovery Museum, take part in the Kayak Kaua'i Day Trips and Adventure Tours, play at the Puakea Golf Course, participate in the Kauai Nature Tours, take a catamaran tour with Catamaran Kahanu, or visit the Koke'e Natural History Museum.

Whalers Cove Oceanfront Condominiums

The Whalers Cove Oceanfront Condominiums along Puuholo Road in Koloa in the island of Kauai in Hawaii are situated on a bluff one mile from Poipu Beach. You may want to use Whalers Cove as a base for exploring the beauty of Kauai at the Spouting Horn Beach Park, Poipu Beach Park, the Old Koloa Town, Wailua Falls, and Hanalei. The Waimea Canyon State Park is only 24 miles away.

Property features

One of the distinctive characteristics of this resort is an orchid garden that surrounds it. An infinity-edge swimming pool and doors made of koa wood make this property unique from other resorts of its kind. All of the suites provide you with views of the Pacific Ocean and this is also true with the swimming pool and the nearby spa tub.

The eastern part of the resort has a stairway going to a cove that has been found to be teeming with marine life and to be safe for snorkeling. For the convenience of guests, a barbecue grill with a picnic area is also located right in front of the ocean. Other features of this property include complimentary beach towels and newspapers, free parking, concierge services, free local telephone calls, elevator, safe-deposit box, and Internet access in public areas for a surcharge.

Recreational activities in the area include snorkeling, golfing, basketball, sightseeing via helicopter or airplane, biking, hiking, tennis, running, whale watching, boating, sailing, rowing, swimming, boogie boarding, and surfing.

Room features

There are 39 available rooms in two buildings that are four stories high. Tropical style decoration is used for the rooms and their unique features are cabinets and doors made of koa wood. Housekeeping services are performed every day. Other features include the following: a ceiling fan; balcony; CD player; cable and/or satellite television; kitchen; coffee maker; microwave oven; sofa bed; clock radio; rollaway beds; ironing board and iron; refrigerator; cooking facilities; patio; second bathroom; extra towels; and hair dryer.

Where to go to eat

This condominium resort does not have its own restaurant but it can make reservations for you in nearby dining places. One such place is the Brennecke's Beach Broiler restaurant in Poipu, which is located next to the beach where you can enjoy salads, sandwiches, steak, pasta, and seafood. Another dining place is Keoki's Paradise restaurant, which is also in Poipu.

Another place where you can go to eat is the Beach House Restaurant, which is also found along the south shore of Kauai and has garnered several awards. You may enjoy pasta, grilled fresh fish, sea scallops, grilled mushroom, salads, and mussels. Another notable restaurant that you might want to try is the Plantation Gardens Restaurant and Bar, which features plantation-style dining with Pacific Rim cuisine.

You may also like to try eating at the Puka Dog restaurant for unique Hawaiian style hotdog sandwiches. Meanwhile, at the Poipu Beach Broiler you may try roasted beef ribs, grilled fish, and pork ribs. At the Tidepools Restaurant along Poipu Road, you may want to taste its seafood specialties, prime rib, fresh fish, and char-broiled steaks.

Westin Princeville Ocean Resort Villas

The Westin Princeville Ocean Resort Villas are located atop the green cliffs in Princeville on the North Shore of the Kauai Island of Hawaii. One of its main features is a restaurant that only offers breakfast. Other key features are the two plunge pools, the main swimming pool, and the children's pool. Golf enthusiasts may enjoy their favorite game at the Prince Golf Course at Princeville at Hanalei or the Makai Golf Course at Princeville at Hanalei.

Important features of this resort

Another key feature of the Westin Princeville Ocean Resort Villas is the use of the WestinWORKOUT Gym that assures you that you can continue taking care of your health and wellness even during your vacation. It provides you with advanced cardiovascular equipment, including the lifecycle exercise bicycles, elliptical cross trainers, treadmills, stair climbers, free weights, resistance tubes, stability balls, and medicine balls.

Because the nearby Sheraton Kauai Resort is also owned by Starwood Hotels, you can enjoy your meal in its restaurants and charge it to your account at the Westin Princeville Ocean Resort Villas. You may also ask for assistance from the concierge for various services such as restaurant reservations, transportation arrangements, and the booking of various tours.

If you have children, you may be pleased to know about the Westin Kids Club, which was designed to provide children whose ages range from five to 12 with the opportunities to participate in activities that make them more aware and knowledgeable about Hawaiian traditions and culture.

As a complimentary service, transportation by shuttle bus is available for free within a radius of 2.5 miles. You can go to nearby places such as the Prince Golf Clubhouse, Princeville Shopping Center, Makai Golf Clubhouse, and Princeville Resort. Other features include: a front desk that is available for 24 hours; bar and lounge; babysitting services; coffee shop; clubhouse; business center; barbecue grills; use of the children's club; valet parking; free parking; safe-deposit box; gift shop; grocery; steam room; sauna; spa tub; and laundry facilities.

Room features

There are 346 available rooms in this two-story property. The standard facilities for the guest villas include a Westin Heavenly Bed with a pillowtop mattress, air conditioning, Internet access, bathroom telephone, bathrobes, cable and satellite television, blackout curtains or drapes, cookware, clock radio, ceiling fan, CD player, designer toiletries, crib when requested, hair dryer, extra towels, electronic keys, DVD player, housekeeping services, handheld shower, voice mail, sitting area, shower and bathtub, microwave oven, makeup mirror, ironing board and iron, kitchen, and lanai.

Where to go to eat

For casual dining, you may prefer to go to the Nanea Restaurant and Bar, which is found on the first floor of the hotel's clubhouse. You are given the choice of dining indoors or outdoors where you can enjoy a view of the Pacific Ocean. Whether to have some quick meals or to purchase some groceries, you can visit the Princeville Market. You can grab some salads, deli sandwiches, side dishes, or baked goods. Meanwhile, at the Wailele Bar, which is conveniently located right next to the main pool, you can enjoy poolside dining and some tropical drinks and other refreshing beverages.

The Point At Poipu

The Point At Poipu is located along the Pe'e Road at Koloa and is close to the southernmost tip of the island of Kauai in Hawaii. It overlooks the Shipwreck Beach and the southernmost tip can provide you with exceptional scuba diving and snorkeling experiences.

Resort features

The Point At Poipu has 215 available suites in 10 buildings ranging in height from two stories to three stories in an area of 22 acres. There are three kinds of vacation areas, where one is located in the middle of the lagoon pool, another is found in the bluff, and the third is designated as the adults-only area. The buildings located at the bluff provide you will unique views of humpback whales during their migration in the winter.

The lagoon swimming pool has a grotto tub on one side and a sandy beach on the other. A gigantic hot tub for adults only had been constructed in a private area that overlooks the Pacific Ocean. A sun deck encircles the hot tub and there are barbecue grills in some areas. Other amenities include: physical fitness equipment; concierge services by a local expert; babysitting services; spa services; poolside bar; Internet access in public areas; safe-deposit box found at the front desk; picnic area; patio; free parking; and ATMs and banking services.

Recreational activities within the area include golfing, volleyball, horse riding, and tennis. Other activities include snorkeling, boating, the use of personal watercraft, fishing, kayaking, sailing, parasailing, boogie boarding, surfing, rafting, mountain biking, hiking, skydiving, and sightseeing by airplane or helicopter.

Room features

The room decorations are based on the Hawaiian style and every suite is provided with a complete kitchen. All rooms have cable and satellite television; CD player; videocassette recorder; video game console; two telephones; carpeted living area; air-conditioned bedrooms; ceiling fans in other rooms; voice mail; balcony; hair dryer; clock radio;

Internet access; pay movies; ironing board and iron; in-room safe; housekeeping services; and crib when requested.

Where to go to eat

When you get hungry you may want to try the Poolside Grill, which is an open-air restaurant that is located right next to the lagoon pool. Breakfast usually consists of Belgian waffles and omelets, while lunch and dinner may offer some salads, sandwiches, hamburgers, pizza, and tropical drinks.

Another place to go for dining is the Poipu Bay Grill and Bar, which is found at Ainako Road, Poipu, Koloa. You can enjoy the beautiful views of the Poipu Bay Golf Course while you are eating. You may also want to try the Tidepools restaurant that offers Hawaiian seafood at the Hyatt Regency Kauai along Poipu Road, Koloa.

If you prefer American cuisine, you can try the Plantation Gardens Restaurant and Bar also at Poipu Road, Poipu, Koloa. The menu is based on the food served in the sugar plantations of Hawaii. All of the vegetables utilized in the menus are organically grown.

Meanwhile, the Beach House Restaurant along Lawai Road, Poipu, Kauai, offers European, Asian, Hawaiian, seafood, and Pacific Rim cuisines for those who like variety.

Pono Kai/Bluegreen Resort

The Pono Kai/Bluegreen Resort is a luxury condominium resort located along the sandy beach at Kuhio Highway in Kapaa in the island of Kauai, Hawaii. It is only half a mile to the Coconut MarketPlace while the Lihue Airport is only 15 miles away. This family-oriented resort occupies an area of 13 acres and provides you with a relaxing environment filled with coconut palms, banana trees, and gardens in this tropical paradise.

Resort features

Only a few steps from the resort are the sandy beaches where you can engage in various activities. Other important features of the resort include free parking; an outdoor swimming pool; suitability of the facilities for children, concierge services; elevator; child care and/or babysitting services; airport transportation; barbecue grills; Internet access in the public areas; tour assistance; microwave oven in the lobby; secure parking; security guard; steam room; spa tub; sauna; picnic area; library; laundry facilities; fitness equipment; multilingual staff; wedding services; limousine service; and video library.

Possible activities within the resort and in the neighborhood include shuffleboard, basketball, volleyball, golf, and croquet. You may also take lessons in lei-making or the hula. You can also participate in luaus and some island excursions. Other recreational and sports activities include fishing, biking, kayaking or canoing, horseback riding, rafting, scuba diving, snorkeling, water skiing, and hiking. You may also go shopping, visit the museums, have a massage at the spa, visit historic sites, or go to the state parks.

Room features

There are 240 available rooms in this condominium resort and they are either of the one-bedroom type or two-bedroom type. All rooms have sofa beds, sitting rooms, and completely equipped kitchens that have stoves, refrigerators, and microwave ovens. High-speed Internet access may be requested with some surcharges.

Other room characteristics at Pono Kai/Bluegreen Resort include the following: air conditioning; access to rooms through exterior corridors; in-room safe; balcony; iron board and iron when requested; cable and satellite television; bathrobes; climate control; CD player; patio; shower and bathtub; telephone; lanai; free toiletries; cookware, utensils and dishes; DVD player; extra towels; videocassette recorder; voice mail; private bathroom; electronic keys; hair dryer; wake-up calls; and ceiling fan.

Where to go to eat

Pono Kai/Bluegreen Resort does not have its own restaurant but there are several places to dine in the Kapaa area. These include the Olympic Cafe Restaurant along the Kuhio Highway for some upscale coffee favorites; the Kintaro Restaurant, which is also found along the Kuhio Highway, for Japanese cuisine; Buzz Restaurant, which is a grill and bar along the Kuhio Highway; Papaya's Natural Food Market, for the casual market and deli, also along Kuhio Highway; and The Shack Sports Bar along Kuhio Highway.

Other dining places in Kapaa include Norberto's El Cafe for Mexican cuisine along the Kuhio Highway; Bubba Burgers also along Kuhio Highway; the Mermaids Restaurant along Kuhio Highway; Scotty's Beachside Bbq Restaurant along Kuhio Highway; the Blossoming Lotus Restaurant along Kukui Street for some vegetarian cuisine; and the Hawaiian Blizzard Restaurant along Kuhio Highway for the best in shaved ice.

East Kauai

Kauai's East Side, known as the "Coconut Coast," is a magical region filled with history and culture. The landscape is filled with coconut trees and it is here that the coconut grove comes to life. Kauai is a very popular tourist destination because of its abounding natural beauty and exciting activities. It's a good idea to book your tour and vacation plans several weeks before to craft that perfect Kauai Vacation.

East Kauai awaits you with its long list of fun and exciting activities, adventures, and escapades. Book your tour and vacation plan several weeks before to ensure a perfect Kauai vacation. Here is a list of the perfect places you can explore while on vacation in East Kauai, as this area also serves as a gateway to attractions in nearby regions.

Sleeping Giant

Explore the natural wonders of the Coconut Coast and be amazed with the "Sleeping Giant," also known as Nounou Mountain. This spectacular mountain is famous for its shape, which looks like a giant slumbering away in Kauai's green eastern side. Legend has it that a giant pestered the village with his huge appetite, making the villagers think of a way to trick the giant and make him sleep.

Bell Stone

Another tourist attraction you should explore when in East Kaui is the Bell Stone. This historical landmark is a reddish stone that produces a unique sound when struck. In ancient times, the birth of a royalty was announced by striking the bell stone. Set against East Kauai's rich landscape, this place offers plenty of photo opportunities.

Fern Grotto

Take that cruise going up to the historic and sacred Wailua River to a lava rock grotto embedded with tropical ferns, and be serenaded by a group of Hawaiian musicians playing traditional Hawaiian songs. The boats found on the south side of the river leave every 30 minutes, and takes about 40 minutes to travel. On the way to Fern Grotto, you get to take all the pictures you want, with you and your loved ones posing behind the grasslands, and with Mt. Waialeale displayed in the background. Remember, cruise boats and kayak rentals are located on the south side of the Wailua River before crossing the bridge.

Wailua

A blessed and significant place highlighted by the Wailua River, this is a river on the island of Kauai. It begins at the crater and is the only river where ferries and boats larger than kayaks can navigate in the Hawaiian Islands. It is a very busy place for the locals and visitors, as it is the center for boat tours to Fern Grotto, kayaking, and water skiing activities. Don't fail to visit this spot and when you go there, and make sure you take advantage of all it has to offer.

Wailua River State Park

It is in this park where you will find the popularly known Lydgate Park, which also showcases several archeological sites, being around since 800 A.D. This place is perfect for snorkeling activities in the beach.

There's also a picnic grove along the rock lagoons where families and kids may swim safely.

Lydgate State Park

Located on the east shore of Kauai, this park is where Hikina Akala (the rising sun) Heiau is situated, which is an ancient temple right at the north end of the beach. If you traveled to Kauai with your family, or if you are still an amateur swimmer, and you badly want to take a plunge into the waters, you can swim here without having to worry too much about your kids because there are lifeguards roaming around the beaches. This is the perfect place if you want a family-friendly destination in this part of Kauai.

Wailua Falls

This is a must-see waterfall in Wailua River State Park, with its majestic 80-foot tiered waterfall. During Wailua Falls' normal flows, it is such a beautiful sight to see the waters dropping in three separate segments. During its high flows, it is even a much stunning view to behold, with its waters doing a single massive fall. Unlike other Kauai waterfalls which will require helicopter tours, the Wailua Falls is very easy to see because it is the most easily accessible waterfall in Kauai. It became famous when it was featured in the opening scenes of the once popular old television show, Fantasy Island. It has been said that many, many years ago, it is also where ancient men used to dive off over the falls to prove their worthiness. The best time to visit Wailua Falls is very early in the morning

Opaekaa Falls

This is yet one of Kauai's beautiful water falls; flowing year-round, unlike other waterfalls in Kauai that depend on heavy rains in order to showcase some stunning waterfalls. You can have wonderful photo opportunities with the Opaekaa Falls as it offers scenic peaks of the Makaleha Mountains on the background and a restored Hawaiian village on the riverbanks. Located in the northern part of the the Wailua River, this fall cannot be reached by river or trail. By just staying at Kuamo'o Road, you will be able to have an excellent and safe view of the waterfalls. The name Opaekaa is a word that means "rolling shrimp," because it's been said that the river used to be swarmed by shrimps rolling and jumping in the turbulent waters just at the bottom of the water falls. These waterfalls can easily be seen overlooking the Kuamo'o Road. The best time for a magnificent view is mid-morning, when the sun complements the natural beauty of the waterfalls.

Keahua Forestry Arboretum

This arboretum is perfect for a relaxing picnic with the family. Nature lovers will definitely fall in love with this place as it boasts plenty of monkeypod, eucalyptus, and mango trees. Aside from picnic tables, the Keahua Forestry Arboretum also offers pools where you can swim around and cool off.

Kapaa Town

After all that tiring nature-tripping adventures, make sure you also find the time to drop by and stroll through Kapaa Town where you can find some nice items, including some great Hawaiian craft pieces, souvenir aloha-print shirts, Hawaiian jewelry, and fine art objects. Some shops also offer life-size paintings of whales on a wall and clock towers which are very unique Hawaiian crafts you can bring home as tokens of your perfect vacation in Kauai.

And when you get hungry after all those breath-taking and exhausting views and trips, make sure you drop by at any of East Kauai's charming restaurants where you will be pampered with sumptuous treats such as steaks, and spoiled with Hawaiian's long and varied list of different favorite treats from vegetarian, Hawaiian, and Asian dishes since these are all part of the Coconut Coast's culinary specialties. The Coconut Coast's dining options offer choices from cozy diners to fancy restaurants. Enjoyable dining includes a visit to a soda shop, having a drink or two from the soda fountain while listening to the jukebox.

To visit East Kauai is one smart decision when having a vacation with your loved ones. So, come and visit Kauai's Coconut Coast and indulge in the beauty and variety this destination offers. Let yourself loose in the quiet splendor of this region's green tropical setting and extraordinary natural heritage. Come and discover the traditional Hawaiian aloha spirit that abounds in this welcoming island paradise. Aside from exploring such awesome spots, East Kauai's Coconut Coast offers to both locals and visitors other adventurous and exciting things to do. So, come and explore the island and pamper yourself in its splendor.

How to Get to East Kauai

You can only arrive at Kauai by air. At 550 square miles, Kauai, the oldest northernmost Hawaiian island, offers its visitors ideal vacation adventures. The Coconut Coast, how the eastern side of Kauai is called, is lined up with coconut palm trees and is one of the most populated commercialized region. There are just so many fun and exciting things to do in the island. So don't fail to stop by the Coconut Coast to see what breathtaking sites await you and your loved ones.

Going to the east of Kauai

Arrival of Kauai visitors is via this laidback island's major airport at Lihue, a small terminal served with inter-island flights by Alaska, American, Delta, Hawaiian, United Airlines, and US Airways, These carriers offer non-stop service from the U.S. West Coast.

Lihue is known to be the business center of Kauai, where most tourist and business activities take place. For a piece of travel tip, always prepare for your air tour to Kauai and flying into Lihue. For the best possible view, select a window seat on the left side of the aircraft. More often than not, landing will take place at the northern side because of trade winds. From this angle, it is impossible for you not to see you the dramatic cliff view every visitor would marvel at during air tours. There is also the deep water port at Nawiliwili for cruise ships. From and to Honolulu, Norwegian Cruise Lines has cruises that take you between the islands.

Modes of transportation

You may avail of air tours in East Kauai to give you the opportunity to see many of the landforms created after the collapse and reconstruction of the island, since the island has experienced catastrophic failures in the past. On the other hand, ground transportation on East Kauai includes rental cars, hotel shuttles, taxis, and mopeds. You also wont't have too much trouble looking for guided tours aboard motor-coaches, four-wheel drive vehicles, mini-buses, vans, and limousines.

Kauai also has limited bus service, but rental car is still the best way to really see the island and the only way to get to some remote and scenic spots. It's good to know that many rental car companies have branches and offices near the Lihue Airport. Car rentals allow for travelers' convenience and flexibility to roam around. All passengers in a vehicle are required to wear a seatbelt and all infants must be strapped into car seats.

Pedestrians always have the right of way, even if they're not in the crosswalk. There are only a few traffic lights necessary to maintain the smooth flow of traffic. This is because everyone follows what they call the "Aloha" traffic customs, that is, driving slow, giving in to others, and avoiding tailgating. Experience the local style of driving when on one-lane bridges. Give way to oncoming traffic when in a one-lane bridge. If you are the oncoming traffic and there is a line waiting on the other side, stop and let the other vehicles cross.

Another option for transportation is the use of bicycles. Plans of developing a major bike path for the east side of the island are underway, as of early 2005. Though there are visible bike paths, most connections between towns are found through the major highways. Eventually, the ins and outs of East Kauai can easily be accessed through exclusive bikeways.

Kauai has two main highways on Kauai, and they both start at Lihue. Through Kaumualii Highway, you can head to the west and go to the towns of Kalaheo, Hanapepe, Waimea, and Kekaha before the Na Pali Coast. Meanwhile, Kuhio Highway is the best route when heading north from Lihue. From this highway, you can go to Kapa`a, Kilauea, Princeville, and Hanalei and reach Na Pali's other side. Either way, you are going to get to East Kauai.

What to Do in East Kauai

Planning a much deserved vacation in Kauai? Why not explore its eastern side known as the Coconut Coast? For sure, there are tourist spots and activities that are unique to this part of the island. Basically, the list of activities will be the same, but the scenic views would make a big difference. If you want to make sightseeing a special activity for you, then you must engage in many underwater activities and even go on tours to see everything up close. From marine exploration to hiking trails, the natural wonders of East Kauai are within reach.

East Kauai is waiting to be explored by you. All you need to do is familiarize yourself with scenic spots in this part of the island and have a good idea of how you can turn your vacation into a memorable island adventure. Aside from accommodations, your itinerary also requires some careful planning. You'll surely find a long list of fun and exciting activities here. Whether you decide to tour with a group or go solo, taking in the island's true wonders is simply rewarding. Discover Kauai and make the most of your stay with the countless adventures you can choose from. Here are a few suggestions:

Ground tours

You may start your East Kauai escapades with ground tours. Enjoy the sun, laze around the grassy fields, and take full advantage of the island's captivating beauty. Strolling in the lush gardens, biking, hiking, and horseback riding are among the things you can do while on tour. Of course, golf enthusiasts surely wouldn't want to miss practicing their swings on East Kauai's golf courses.

Mountain biking

Discovering the Coconut Coast by biking is like hitting two birds with one stone. You get to exercise while you discover the real splendor of the island. You can choose to bike effortlessly on paved roads or moderately for in-between places. Also watch out for those sharp curves, where it's steep and the stops are abrupt.

For amateur bikers, they should enjoy the ride on evenly leveled roads to make it easier for them to get around the island. While biking, you will get the chance to see Kauai landmarks such as the Wailua Falls along the Ma'alo Road, sandy beaches that stretch from east to west, and the Spalding Monument. Just make sure that you always wear your protective biking gear to avoid untoward incidents. The scenic ride will surely take you closer to the Coconut Coast's attractions at a leisurely pace.

Hiking

Don't miss the chance to go hiking on East Kauai trails. You may get some maps from the Department of Land and Natural Resources and the Division of State Parks to make it easier for you to get around this part of the island. Travelers are well advised to indulge in this physical activity. Although tiring, the scenic view, fresh air, and peaceful surrounding will make it worth your while. Majority of Kauia's territory is not accessible by road, so hiking is definitely one way of touring the island up close while maintaining your physical fitness. Be sure to prepare before hiking; bear in mind all of the safety tips and guidelines for this strenuous but exciting activity.

To avoid getting lost and to learn more about the island attractions, it's best to go on tour. The tour guide will surely make the trip more enjoyable by giving you insights on different landmarks and tourist spots. This is also recommended for group travelers.

Exciting water adventures

The eastern part of Kauai also offers a wide arrray of fun and exciting water adventures. You may join boat tours on the island and savor the magnificent spatter of the ocean while cruising and sailing with your loved ones. If you have kids with you, they will surely enjoy and never forget the other thrilling water escapades, such as whale watching, fishing, diving, and snorkeling.

Snorkeling

The Coconut Coast has various locations for snorkeling, thanks to its calm and cool waters. Amateur snorkeling enthusiasts should choose a shallow area for this water activity. They can go to Anini Beach while in East Kauai, which has been proven safe for beginners. Poipu Beach Park is another area that offers good snorkeling spots, while other beach parks are also known for their colorful tropical fish that makes snorkeling all the more exciting.

For experienced snorklers, though, there are the reefs of Kee Beach and Haena Beach Park, which are very well known snorkeling spots in this part of the island. There is also the Tunnels Beach in Haena, with a reef that's just perfect for snorkeling adventures. Make sure, though, that you check first the current of the waters to ensure safe underwater activity. You should also do your share in preserving these coral reefs. Make sure that you won't destroy any natural habitat or disturb the marine creature.

Kayak and paddling tours

As soon as you set foot on East Kauai, prepare yourself for some action-packed kayaking activity in the island. Hire a professional guide when kayaking along the Wailua River. There are cruise boats and kayak rentals on its south side. You can also cross the bridge to the popular Fern Grotto, a lava rock grotto embedded with tropical ferns. Or, if you wish to kayak for a much longer time, then you should try the Hanalei River, which is one of the longest kayaking paths that pass through Kauai's plains. You can also take a peek at Kalihiwai, which showcases its own superb scenery.

Scuba diving

Divers, whether amateur or professional, will definitely take pleasure in Kauai as a diving location, since the island presents loads of sites to scuba dive. The island offers dives ranging from boat dives, night dives, and other various dive tours that offer an exciting discovery of the abundant ocean life, such as tropical fish and reef creatures, dolphins, and sea turtles. Diving gear and other diving equipment may also be rented in the island, if you did not bring yours. Or, if you wish to buy one, there are several dive shops in East Kauai.

If you're an experienced diver, you might as well take your gripping dives on the east shores of Kauai, while those who are amateurs in the turf of diving should start with designated sites for beginners. Kauai even boasts of having caves and lava tubes, which can be stimulating diving targets for the more advanced or professional divers. The island bestows certifications on anyone who wants to get certified, as long as he or she has a medical paperwork to present.

Whale watching tours
Don't miss the fun of watching whales come out of the water in East Kauai's shores. You can catch a glimpse of the whales also in various parts of the island such as the Kilauea Point National Wildlife Refuge, the Kalalau Trail on the North Shore, Kukui O Lono Park at Kalaheo, and Poipu Beach. It's more amusing, though, if you watch these water creatures while on a boat tour since you can come closer to the whales while they jump out of the water, making the experience much more intimate. No need to bring binoculars. If you want to do this

particular activity, schedule your vacation from late November through early May for the peak season for whale watching.

Shopping on the island

Before you end hopping throughout the east of Kauai, be sure to drop by their small souvenir shops and malls. You can purchase several unique souvenir items to bring home such as Aloha shirts, jewelry, home and personal accessories, and some works of art.

The eastern side of Kauai presents a variety of fun shops and eateries. There is Lihue and the Kalapaki area, which offer country stores, fine art shops, gift shops, and farmers' markets, where you can buy loads of stuff to bring home including soaps, paintings, apparel, coffee, Kukui guava jams, fabrics, and many other collectible items. Should you get starved after a tiring day, go to the Wailua Shopping Plaza that houses several restaurants for sumptuous Hawaiian food.

There is also the Coconut Marketplace, which is an umbrella venue for 70 shops selling precious Hawaiian souvenirs, fine works of art, various antiques, jewelry, craft items, and so much more. Also, don't miss going to Kapaa Town and Kinipopo Shopping Village where you can find the best buys for various Aloha shirts, vintage maps, fine art, and jewelry for your loved ones back home.

Where to Stay in East Kauai

If you're planning to have a vacation in East Kauai and you're looking for accommodations, there are so many choices to choose from. East Kauai offers its visitors with an array of choices as to where to stay in Kauai. It's truly not an easy task choosing a place where you can stay and dine, since there are so many options to choose from in this Garden Island. There are the luxury resort hotels, the condominium type of accommodations, and the economy rooms for budget-friendly accommodations.

The most populated towns such as Kapa'a and Lihu'e comprise the eastern shore. Kapa'a is centrally located and so if you will stay in a hotel there, you will be able to view the best of both worlds; the sugar cane plantations of the south shore, and the taro fields of the northern shore. If you're looking for luxury resort hotels to stay in, then you should head off to Kapaa, Kauai.

Kapaa luxury resort hotels

Kauai Coast Resort

If you wish to stay somewhere with a resort condominium ambience, then head off to the Kauai Coast Resort at the Beachboy in Kapaa. This magnificent resort condominium, after having been refurbished for millions of dollars, now boasts of a lagoon swimming pool designed with unique rock arrangments, a children's pool, an oceanside Jacuzzi, and cascading waters featured as a background at the main entrance. The Kauai Coast Resort is a hotel that offers a total of 108 units with ocean views, with all amenities and services geared towards ensuring a perfect stay for its visitors. So, book now, and discover the aloha service in Kauai.

Lanikai Resort

The Lanikai Resort, still in Kapaa, is a resort condo suite built in 1982 and reconstructed in 1993. It is also considered to be a superbly large condo suite located amidst beautifully landscaped green gardens. It remains an absolutely private spot, while visitors enjoy the resort's white sandy beach. It is very convenient for the visitors to roam around and shop, since the suite is just a walking distance away from the buzz of restaurants and shops. So, if you plan to hang out at the beach while at the same time and then do your quick shopping for souvenirs afterwards, or if you do not have sufficient time to dine out in far away establishments, then the Lanikai Resort is for you.

Fern Grotto Inn

Another resort inn in Kapaa is the Fern Grotto Inn, located in Hawaii's largest coconut grove near Coco Palms Resort. Located in the center of Kapaa, Fern Grotto Inn's just a very short drive away when going to the restaurants and shopping stores, and to many of the beaches of Kauai, as well as its abundant state parks. If you choose to stay in Fern Grotto, it will be easier for you to explore Kauai, going to its hiking trails, and historic sites. Also, a short drive will take you to two beautiful waterfalls, which you should not dare miss. Fern Grotto is a perfect place to go kayaking, because Fern Grotto is located in Waialua River, which can only be reached either by kayaking or a short hike. The river then brings you near the majestic Kauai waterfalls.

Fern Grotto Inn offers vacation rental cottages with beautiful amenities guaranteed to make your Hawaiian vacation a perfect and unforgettable getaway. Come, experience, and discover why first-time travelers return and frequent the island once they have visited Kauai. If you really want relaxation and peace, you will surely enjoy the very laid-back atmosphere here at Fern Grotto Inn, what with the sandy shores of nearby beaches and the very near Lydgate Park, which is just a five-minute stroll from your cottage. Drive for three minutes, and you'll see the breathtaking view of the Opaekaa Falls. Truly, it's a total package altogether, staying at Fern Grotto Inn.

Lihue hotels
Lihue, on the other hand, offers a combination of luxury and economy hotels. Many visitors opt to stay in the area of Lihue due to its

proximity to the island's largest airport, which is just a few minutes away from the town. A popular hotel in Lihue is the Kauai Marriott Resort & Beach Club, showcasing Kauai's white beaches and sapphire lagoons. It is a 10-floor hotel with modern amenities perfect for vacationers. What is there to ask for if there's already a long queue of restaurants to dine in, a fitness center to keep you fit, several shopping centers, and exciting physical activities such as kayaking and surfing? Book now for a more perfect holiday vacation.

Another prominent hotel in Lihue is the Hilton Kauai Beach Resort. It has three adult pools, water slides, as well as children's pools. The best thing about this hotel is even when you're on vacation, you may still carry out your work should the need arise, because the hotel offers business amenities including a very spacious conference room, and its business center, which is equipped with fax and copy and print services. As for the rooms, they were made with Hawaiian designs, and are overlooking the ocean.

Budget-friendly accommodations
Kauai Sands Hotel
Other usual picks of hotels and luxury resorts on the Coconut Coast include the Sands Hotel. This was named as such because of the beach's peculiar white sand blending with its neatly landscaped lawns in the ocean-fronting eight acres of property located at the Coconut

Coast of Kauai. The Sands Hotel can accommodate its visitors with its 250 rooms, and is just a walking distance from the Coconut Marketplace, an open-air market very renowned for its unique shops and restaurants. The Coconut Marketplace also offers free Polynesian entertainment every night.

Marc Pono Kai Resort

The Marc Pono Kai Resort Hotel is about 13 acres of tropical property converted into a hotel. It is a sure favorite choice of travelers when staying in Kauai, due to its big space, not to mention its ocean-fronting feature which delights everyone staying in the hotel. It offers great ambiance for families to get together, presenting various daily activities for everyone.

Hale Lani Bed & Breakfast and the Marriott Resort and Beach Club

For other options when it comes to affordable accommodations, you can stay at the Hale Lani Bed & Breakfast, where the rooms are incorporated with their own kitchens, private entrances and patios, and two out of their four units have hot tubs. Or you may wish to try the three-star Kauai Marriott Resort and Beach Club where you can lounge poolside and take in the vista of the neighboring Nawiliwili Bay. Rooms here are not so heavy on your pocket, so you'll definitely have some leftover money to shop for some souvenirs to bring home. Plus, the quality of the service here makes the vacation more memorable.

East Kauai is perfect for travelers with or without a big budget. With all the accommodation options you can choose when planning to stay in this region, you're sure to find one that's perfect for your budget and needs. To make things easier when looking for an accommodation, surf the net for accommodation listings that offer special deals and discount rates. You can also look for online tours or packages that already include accommodations and transportation for more savings. If you don't mind splurging, many travel sites offer packages for luxury resorts and hotels in East Kauai. For frequent stays at this region, vacation rentals may be a better option. Aside from hotels, resorts, inns, and bed and breakfasts, there are plenty of vacation rentals found here. There are one-bedroom, budget-friendly vacation rentals if you're budget-conscious. As for luxury vacation rentals, they can include five-bedroom units with amazing ocean views.

Fixed Budget

If you wish to travel but your budget seems inadequate, don't worry. Kauai offers its beauty and majesty not only to travelers who can afford to pay for the high rates of luxury resort hotels, but also to travelers with limited finances. There are so many promotions on Kauai tours, making the prices very affordable to travelers. The key here is you should research and choose cheap accommodations, rental services, and places in East Kauai that offer lots of fun and exciting things to do that won't require a big budget.

A mere look at East Kauai's shores all lined up with coconut palms will tell you why this place is called the "Coconut Coast." By just staring at the line of coconut trees set against the clear blue waters of East Kauai's beaches, you'll definitely be inspired by the natural beauty this place is known for. You don't really need a huge amount of money to be able to admire and experience the beauty of Kauai, its azure oceans, and its breath-taking views. Well, if you are looking for a budget-friendly East Kauai accommodation, an affordable adventure, or a restaurant that offers quality food without the high price tags, below are some suggestions.

Affordable accommodations in East Kauai

Anahola Sun Beach Rentals
The price of this accommodation is a great value considering that this place is just right for large groups or families who want to have their own privacy. Boasting of rooms with ocean views, this destination is truly an island paradise. A central courtyard offers more privacy,

especially if you want a place to reflect and enjoy the serene environment.

Beach House Kauai Hostel

For those traveling on very strict budgets, choosing to stay in the Beach House Kauai Hostel is a good decision. The hostel is located in a quiet area close to various establishments such as Internet cafes, grocery stores, and very affordable restaurants. Guests are endowed with attractive, comfortable rooms, and a private double bed for each. To cut on further expenses, instead of dining out, you may prepare some food for a picnic at the picnic area. The area is already equipped with amenities such as barbeque grills, rooftop showers and restrooms, live entertainment, and a common kitchen and parking as well. You don't need to rent cars anymore since there are also several nearby attractions including Ho'olalaea Waterfalls, Nounou Mountain, and the Keahua Forestry Arboretum and Kalapaki Beach.

Kauai Sands Hotel

Sands Hotel is yet another condominium tendering a good price deal for all travelers. It is a very short walking distance from the majestic Wailua Falls, so you don't need to rent cars to roam around, or avail of tours just to see it, because everything seems so near to Wailua Falls when staying at Sand's Hotel. If you are sticking on a strict budget, you may begin your tours by walking along the beautiful white sand beaches of Kauai. You savor the heat of the sun, feel the white grains of sand on your feet, and get the chance to stroll with the Hawaiian monk seals that frequent the shores to also have their taste of the sun.

Sightseeing at the waterfalls

This part of Kauai is known for its majestic waterfalls that remind you of an era when Hawaii was still a young island. Enjoying the view from spectacular points is definitely a budget-friendly activitiy you can do in East Kauai. Whether you're with your friends or with your family, the waterfalls of East Kauai should definitely be included in your must-see list.

Hiking and rock climbing

You may try the various hiking trails of East Kauai, such as the trail going to the top of the Sleeping Giant. Experience how nothing will compare to the fulfillment you will feel upon gazing at the surrounding valleys of the Coconut Coast, or the eastern shore without having to spend so much.

Rock climbing is also an exciting activity to do with your loved ones. Although some of the trails are very challenging, it is worth the exhaustion, especially when you see the top view, which is an absolutely breath-taking view of the sea-side cliffs.

Water adventures

There are also cheap but exciting water adventures in East Kauai. You can sign up for a snorkel tour that already includes your lunch. Or, better yet, save your extra money by just renting a mask and fins at activity wholesalers in Hanalei. After which, grab a sandwich or plate lunch for extra savings.

Other activities which will give you the same satisfaction without costing you a single penny is by taking nature walks and strolls in the tropical greens of Kauai. These can lead to discoveries of the hidden valleys and amazing waterfalls. Aside from the fact that you won't have to spend a penny when enjoying the beautiful environment of East Kauai, you'll be getting that needed exercise after munching on delicious Hawaiian delicacies.

As for watching cultural shows without having to spend anything, there are those in East Kauai. Many hotels present hula performances for free, torch lighting ceremonies, and lei making classes. Just drop by the Coconut Marketplace in Kapaa to get a glimpse of Kauai's popular cultural events for free.

Best cheap restaurants in East Kauai

Travelers staying in East Kauai for a vacation, as well as the local people of Kauai, just adore the Coconuts Island Style Grill. It has become a long-time favorite because this restaurant offers to its guests lots of great food at affordable prices.

Another great place to dine is the Garden Island BBQ & Chinese Restaurant. Guests will love this restaurant as it offers sumptuous local Chinese food marked at very low prices. Along with a remarkably friendly crew, the Garden Island BBQ is surely an all-time favorite of both Kauai guests and locals.

One more amazingly affordable place to eat that always surprises people is the Hamura Saimin Stand. The food here is incredibly affordable and superbly flavorful. The saimin served here is said to be one of the best on the island, so if you are in Lihue, Kauai, then make sure you don't leave Kauai without having a taste of the Hamura Saimin Stand.

And lastly, it's a must that you try Hawaii's ever so popular "plate lunch." You don't only pay for the great food served to you, but also for the cultural experience that's enriching for the guests ordering the plate lunch. A plate lunch includes a choice of potato or macaroni salad, two scoops of rice, and a meat entréc. Delectable choices for the entrée' include Teriyaki beef, Korean-style ribs, kalua pig and cabbage, pork katsu, fresh caught mahimahi or opakapaka, beef stew, or a curry dish. There are many combinations of dishes to choose from. Remember, never leave Kauai without indulging in their plate lunch. This is definitely one experience you will never forget.

Many restaurants throughout the island of Kauai and Hawaii in general offer plate lunch specials, making them an affordable option for those who want to taste the local delicacies of Hawaii without busting their budget. Plus, because the servings are usually generous, you'll certainly feel filled after having a plate lunch.

Cheap accommodations in an astonishingly beautiful island, with countless activities that will not even hurt your pocket, and great food tendered to you at very affordable prices -- what more can a traveler ask for? So, come now to Kauai and have that perfect vacation now.

North Kauai

The North Shore of Kauai is found at the oldest island of Hawaii. This isolated paradise not only lets you take a peek at its cinematic panorama, but also offers you a great number of adventures. The island of Kauai is composed of only two major highways that is why it's very easy to go from the north shore down to its beaches of shimmering white sand. Be ready for rains, though, because when you go to the northern shore of Kauai, you'll experience what it's like to stay at the rainiest part of the island.

Because of the weather, Kauai's landscape are lush, giving it the nickname "The Garden Island." However, the rains shouldn't prevent you from enjoying your vacation at North Shore because the weather is predictable.

Staying one week or one month in Kauai is going to be one memorable experience, so make sure you're ready to capture every moment with your camera. Deciding on which among the astonishing locations in the northern shore of Kauai to visit is a difficult task. So consider your interests very well and plan where you will go. To help you out, here's a list of places to explore:

Hanalei Bay and town of Hanalei

The beautiful Hanalei Bay, popularly described as a crescent beach, is great for a walk, dip, or a game of frisbee. It also offers white sand beaches and some of the best waves on the planet for surfing, making this an enjoyable spot for surfers. This spot also offers other fun and exciting outdoor activities such as snorkeling and hiking. Surely, if you visit North Kauai, you will also fall under its spell like every traveler who's been there. That's why Hanalei Bay is considered one of the most stunning tourist destinations in the world. The water is so clear here you can actually see the fish swimming and even the coral yards underneath.

In Hanalei, you will find the Waioli Mission House, a very historical place made of coral limestone that was built in 1837 by the very first missionary who set foot on Kauai. There is also the Makana Peak, a witness to the ancient tradition of throwing burning spears into the wind up into the sky, and to land in the ocean. Walking through this town is a very fascinating and memorable experience you shouldn't miss. So, make sure you squeeze it in your schedule.

Anini Beach

Anini Beach is one of the safest beaches in Kauai and one of the most protected along the North Shore of the island. What's amazing is that the water on one side of this beach is only four feet deep, gradually flowing to about 100 feet deep on the other side. Kids are safe to swim in the shallow waters while the adults can snorkel in the adjacent reefs. You may also go camping in the park, or watch polo matches held across the street during summer and spring. Anini Beach, just like Kee Beach, is a tourist and family-friendly destination. If you take a plunge, you'll definitely feel as if your swimming in a paradise. The motion picture "Honeymoon in Vegas" was actually filmed in this scenic spot of Kauai.

Kee Beach

If you want to enjoy a strikingly beautiful tropical panorama and incredible sunsets, Kee Beach of North Kauai is the place to go. It even offers a snorkeling lagoon of clear blue water teeming with reef fish known for their vibrant shades, and other colorful forms of marine life such as sluggish sea turtles. Kids and snorkelers will surely enjoy plunging into the waters on a calm day. However, swimming outside the reef might be dangerous since there are sometimes strong currents as well. Also, come early when planning to go to Kee Beach because parking slots are so limited since this spot entertains so many guests most of the time.

Tunnels Beach

Another source of pride of Kauai is the Tunnels beach, located 8 miles from Princeville, and is also referred to as Makua, which is considered to be one of the premier dive sites in the world. Tunnels Beach is a jumble of coral formations, lava tubes, tunnels, and arches, and is home to multicolored species of marine life. There's even a shallow reef that's very safe for kids. Tunnels Beach is truly a tropical bliss and a sure treat for snorkeling fanatics and scuba diving enthusiasts. However, bear in mind that to scuba dive in Kauai, you should have taken professional classes administered by licensed or certified professionals. If you're an amateur diver, simply join a class for a refresher on scuba diving basics.

To reach Tunnels Beach, follow Highway 560 east from Hanalei going to Ha'ena. After passing right through two short rocky roads and a little bit past over Mile Marker #8, you will already see the parking area for the beach. Remember though that you need to come early as there are limited parking slots in the area. Or better yet, you may just drive up to the Haena Beach parking and walk down the shore to Tunnels, and enjoy the stroll.

Na Pali Coast
Na Pali Coast is a world-famous tourist destination in the island of Kauai, what with its breath-taking cliffs rising about 4,000 feet. This spot was the very first region in the island that was populated by the native Hawaiians and is believed to be a mystical area where spirits play tricks on travelers visiting this region. There are a lot of fun activities you can do in the Na Pali Coast. You may do horseback riding on the cliffs of this coast for a breath-taking experience, or simply witness the coast's unpopulated cliffs and valleys. Travelers may also choose to get a peek of this coastline by kayaking, taking a tour in an inflatable boat or catamaran, or by taking a helicopter or airplane tour. Truly, the physical exquisiteness of the North Shore will affect

you in as much as the locals' aloha spirit has affected your arrival and visit to the island.

Princeville Resort

If you travel more to the north, you will see the very lavish Princeville Resort sitting on a flat terrain leading to the low cliffs at the ocean's rim. Princeville boasts of its own shopping center, stylish homes and condominiums, tennis courts, a fitness center and health spa, as well as resort accommodations while offering a peek of the fabulously clear waters of the oceans, as well as a magnificent view of the mountains. This is also where Hawaii's two most popular and top-rated golf courses, the Prince and Makai Golf Courses, are located. These are some of the jewels in Princeville Resort's crown as one of the popular locations in Kauai.

And if you're the type to party and have some drinks at night, there are some entertaining places in Princeville that you can go to and have some cocktails. The Princevill Restaurant & Bar within Princeville Hotel is a bar that is well-known in the area, offering great ambiance, magnificent views, and the familiar aloha greetings of the friendly Hawaiian locals.

Truly, the locals of Kauai, Hawaii, can truly take pride in themselves for their beloved island of Kauai being one of the most outstanding travel destinations in the world. The more tropical north shore beaches are framed by dark green tree-covered mountains, while the beaches seem like deserts with their golden sand. There are quite a number of splendid beaches in North Kauai, and they are all so easy to find, so plan your vacation to North Kauai months ahead for a spectacular vacation you won't forget.

How to Get to North Kauai

Most travelers would probably be busy listing down all the wonderful sights to explore in North Kauai. For sure, they have given their accommodations some careful thought after going over all the possible options. And yet, they may miss out on one important detail that will affect not only their budget but also the entire trip to Kauai's North Shore. How exactly can they get to North Kauai?

Flying directly

Flying directly is still the best option if you can't wait to set foot on this island. It would save you and your travel companions a two-hour layover in Honolulu (plus a connecting flight to the island). Direct service to Kauai is offered by United Airlines from the west coast, while American Airlines has non-stop daily flights from LA. Direct flights coming from Phoenix are offered by America West, while SunTrips has charters from Oakland International Airport at least once a week. One of the popular travel companies, Pleasant Hawaiian Holidays, has a set of low-cost fare or package deals. They have two weekly non-stop flights coming from San Francisco and Los Angeles. This is in partnership with American Trans Air.

The other airlines land on Honolulu, where passengers have to connect to a half-hour inter-island voyage to Lihue Airport in Kauai. There are two inter-island carriers: Aloha Airlines and Hawaiian Airline. There would be times when the airlines would handle reservations for the connecting flight to Kauai as part of the package cost. If you want to handle them yourself, you could save some dollars by availing of inter-island coupons.

Going on a cruise to North Kauai

Actually, there is not a particular boat that could fetch you from an island and bring you straight to Kauai, but a number of cruises through the islands would make a stop in Kauai. If you'd rather go on a Hawaiian cruise, expect that you won't get to spend too much time on each island. You'd probably be in for some island-hopping.

Fighting that jet lag

Even the most experienced travelers suffer from jet lag. When you travel from north to south, the sluggish feeling you would get (and the other symptoms) would be because of the overall stress of the air journey. Traveling from east to west, in this case, your body gets confused regarding time. From your digestion to other activities in your body, they'd probably all get "out of sync."

Let us give you some crucial tips on how to combat this very inconvenient jet lag:

Adjust your watch to the destination time even before the journey.
Take in lots of water prior, during, and after the journey.
Sleep well days before the flight.
While sampling wine on board is a special experience, getting drunk is a terrible idea.

Landing at Lihue

From Lihue Airport, you may want to hail a taxi or drive a rental car to downtown Lihue (two miles from the airport) and other towns leading to North Shore Kauai. This is because there's no public transportation here. There are also no shuttle vans in the airport. You'll do better with a map that can serve as your guide to the connecting roads and highways of North Shore, Kauai. Before you get behind the wheels, at least plot the best route to your destination or call your hotel for instructions.

Departing from the airport

Agricultural screening is strict here. Both passengers and all baggage going to the mainland would be screened prior to boarding. The following would be confiscated in relation to fruit fly control: fresh avocados, mangoes, bananas, and other local products. If you want to bring processed foods such as coffee or macadamia nuts, there is nothing to worry about. They would be permitted to pass.

What to Do in North Kauai

The north shore of Kauai is just bursting with a variety of fun and thrilling activities along its 552 square miles of land. Kauai, the fourth largest island of the Hawaiian Islands, offers tremendously exhilarating adventures both in ground and in water, and even on air with its helicopter and plane tours. Be ready when you go to North Kauai for the surprisingly spectacular sights you'll see in the region, from sandy beaches to exquisite landscapes, as well as the dynamic and energizing activities you can do here such as surfing, biking, boogie boarding, hiking, kayaking, and horseback riding. Here's a list of adventures you can experience in North Kauai and where you can experience them.

Sailing, snorkeling, rafting, and hiking at Napali Coast

Sail into the breezy yet calm waters of Napali Coast and let nature show you her true beauty. While onboard the boat, you can just laze around and soak some rays or chat with the captain and the crew for a more enriching experience. You can also try snorkeling after your sailing adventure so that you can see for yourself the various marine life that make Kauai a real tropical paradise. To make your vacation more unforgettable, join a rafting tour to Napali Coast. Explore sea caves and be amazed at the spectacular sights you'll see above and under the crystal clear blue waters of the Napali Coast. Make sure to book your rafting tours with reliable touring companies that offer high-quality inflatable rafts or zodiacs.

On land, another way to experience this part of North Kauai is through hiking. Known for its rugged landscapes and challenging terrain, the Napali Coast is the perfect spot for hikers and adventure-seekers. One of the most popular hiking trails in this area is the Hanakapi'ai Trail. This path leads to a sandy beach and lush greenery that'll make the entire trip worthwhile. Just be careful though as this trail gets more tricky during

Kayaking at Napali Coast

The island of Kauai is the only Hawaiian island that has traversable rivers fitting for all types of kayaking. It is very much safe especially that its volcanoes have long been considered dormant for about 5 million years. Kayaking is not just a popular water sport; it's a truly mesmerizing and revitalizing experience that you shouldn't miss.

Whether you prefer river kayaking or ocean kayaking, kayaking tours or kayak eco-tours give you the same exact feeling of fulfillment. You can do kayaking in Kauai and join the Na Pali Coast kayaking tours, or go on kayaking trips through Kauai's rainforests and jungles or waterfalls by choosing the best kayak outfits in the area.

You may do ocean kayaking along Kauai's spectacular Napali Coast, but this is only recommended for those above 16 and are physically fit to perform such an activity. The ocean kayaking tours on Napali coast are truly amazing wonders of nature. However, reserve your kayaking adventures for the calmer months when the giant surfs have already subsided. If you are not the extremely adventurous type of kayaker, go for the gentle flowing rivers that never lead to the rapids. Savor the experience of tying your own kayak at streams' rims while going hiking to have a plunge into the bottom of the beautiful waterfalls.

Surfing adventures at Hanalei Bay

You may take surfing lessons at Hanalei Bay, a crescent beach with the sandy type of bottom, great for taking surfing lessons in Hawaii. It will surely be a safe and fun experience for you and your kids. And more importantly, they only employ surf instructors who are lifeguard certified to ensure safety of all surfing visitors. The Instructor will also give lessons on line surf boards and leashes. Your instructors will make sure you have fun while you surf.

North Kauai eco-tours at Kilauea Point National Wildlife Refuge

Be guided by eco-tourist guides who can share with you their knowledge about the history and wildlife species unique to the garden island of Kauai. Refuge tours will let you marvel at seabirds that make this part of Kauai their home. It's best to visit this place during the nesting season so that you can see the birds go on a hunt for a mate and feed their young ones.

A stroll at the Na `Aina Kai Botanical Gardens

Don't forget to add to your list of places to visit one of the world's most unique botanical gardens, the Na 'Aina Kai, or "Lands by the Sea." This is truly a plant lover's paradise, with more than 70 sculptures made of bronze, making it one of the biggest collections in the country. It is a 240-acre tropical paradise consisting of 13 different and overflowing gardens, a plantation featuring hardwoods, a majestic canyon covered with lush ferns and mosses, and a perfect sandy beach nestled by a meadow and the azure Pacific waters.

Bring the kids along and let them have fun at the "Under the Rainbow," a children's garden that features a beautiful sculpture capturing a scene from the Jack and the Beanstalk fairy tale. A kid-friendly pool awaits the keiki who want to have some fun under the sun. Aside from the pool, kids will surely love the covered wagon and the tropical jungle with is a mix of slides, tunnels, and bridges. Whether you're visiting the place for a family tour or are celebrating the birthday of a young one, this is the place to be if you want your kids to have a more memorable experience at North Kauai.

Zip line tours at the Princeville Ranch Adventures

Another very thrilling and very popular activity in Kauai is ziplining. Book your tour in advance as these tours easily get filled up fast. One North Shore facility that offers ziplining tours is the Princeville Ranch Adventures. Situated in the charming town of Hanalei, the Princeville Ranch Adventures offer a one-of-a-kind zipline tour across the tropical rainforests of Kauai and stunning waterfalls. The tour may also include a cooling dip at one of the waterfalls and a picnic to revitalize you and get you started on your next adventure. An adventure spot spanning a total of 2500 acres, you'll experience the best of North Shore with utmost privacy.

Dolphin watching at North Kauai's shores

Around Hawaii, there are four varieties of dolphins frequenting the waters. However, the two most popular species of dolphins located in Hawaiian waters are the bottlenose dolphins and the spinner dolphins.

Until now, it is not known why the dolphins spin, but just watching the dolphins spin is really a great treat especially for your kids. Spinner dolphins are the smallest of Hawaii's common dolphins, about 5 to 6 ft. long. During the day, they break up into smaller groups and come near the shore to rest and play. The coasts of Napali is one of their favorite playgrounds. The amazing bottlenose dolphins are appreciated for their inshore habits, playfulness around vessels, and star performances at oceanariums.

It's such a fulfilling experience to watch the dolphins happily play in their habitats since these creatures possess an impressive ability to learn and imitate people's behaviors. Visitors who have watched say there's no better animal encounter than with the very intelligent dolphins.

Truly, North Kauai has only to offer the best of everything that's why it's called a paradise in an island. This part of Kauai can boast of its world-class beaches, waterfalls, mountains, and and scenic coastal view points. So, plan your vacation details now and when you get to Kauai, just relax and have fun. Even if you have been to this island paradise before, you will surely keep coming back

Where to Stay in North Kauai

If you are going to stay in North Shore, Kauai, consider first which locations and spots you wish to visit so you can find a suitable place for accommodation. The magnificently green North Shore offers various types of lodging, ranging from luxury hotels to economy rooms. You may also consider getting a vacation rental home, which is common in the island of Kauai.

In the "Garden Isle," it's been said that you'll easily find vacation homes and condominiums that can be rented for a limited stay. Vacation rentals are more suited for families, groups of friends, or several visitors looking for a getaway place. In fact, they have gotten trendier these days. They are sprawled along those wonderful locations in North Kauai. Many visitors actually prefer staying in oceanfront locations.

Here are some suggestions when planning to stay in Kauai's North Shore:

Princeville Resort Hotel
Overlooking Hanalei Bay and the famed "Bali Hai" on Kauai's northern shore, the Princeville Resort is a common choice for oceanfront hotels among tourists. This well designed resort hotel offers around 252 rooms and suites for your accommodation, while at the same time offering a wide range of activities for their guests. There's scuba

diving, snorkeling, surfing, swimming, body boarding, fishing, golf, and hiking. Guests are also given time for meditation or relaxation, and they can also enjoy shopping, dining, and mere sightseeing.

It has four restaurants as well as lounges for gourmet dining and entertainment. You will never starve in Princeville as there are so many restaurants to choose from. Here are just a few to satisfy your hunger and cravings:

* The Beach Restaurant & Bar
This bar caters lunch and snacks anytime you want them. It even offers a poolside luau with Polynesian amusement held every Mondays and Thursdays in the evening.

* Cafe Hanalei
If you want a hearty meal for breakfast, lunch, or dinner, make sure you drop by Cafe Hanalei. Among its specialties are champagne Sunday brunch and seafood buffet of continental dishes.

* La Cascata
This resto is known for its quaint atmosphere, with its terra-cotta floors and trompe l'oeil paintings. It's recommended for guests who want to sample Mediterranean cuisine with a little bit of island flavor.

* The Living Room

Still in Princeville Resort, you might want to relax with some afternoon teas or some drinks served with hors d'oeuvres for your siesta. It is so fascinating to stay there because you can see the best view of the sunset while trying to get some rest and relaxation.

If you're with a special someone, you may treat her to a romantic dinner by the sea at the Princeville Resort, where they will serve you a five-course gourmet menu. You will definitely win each other's hearts for sure.

When looking for a place to stay, might as well consider your dining options. Here in North Kauai, you shouldn't dare miss the real Hawaiian treats.

Other choices for accommodation

The Westin Princeville Ocean Resort Villas
This resort has hundreds of standard guest rooms; you are given the chance to choose which type of view you would prefer. There are units that overlook the ocean, while some rooms are sure to give you vistas of the high mountain or garden views. It's a haven where you can rest and relax, perfect for honeymooners and great for golfers.

The villas are beautifully designed with modern amenities and a private lanai. You will definitely feel the Hawaiian warmth in its friendly and capable staff. Also, these villas are not separate villas, but are quite similar to condominium units fronting the oceans for a magnificent view. The resort features 173 two-bedrooms and 173 suites, four pools, a two-story clubhouse, a restaurant, and a store where you can buy your basic necessities. During dry weather, guests usually stroll along the Anini Beach, since the resort lies just 200 feet above it.

Where to eat in Westin Princeville? Nanea Restaurant and Bar seems to be the favorite choice of guests here. Enjoy some Hawaiian treats while watching the waves slapping through the ocean. Nanea Restaurant serves breakfast buffet, continental breakfast, and a la carte, depending on your choice. This is from 6:30 until 10:30 in the morning. It also serves lunch menu from 11 in the morning to 2 in the afternoon. Savory steaks and seafood dishes are also served for dinner from 5:30 in the afternoon to 9 in the evening.

Wailua Bay View Condominiums

Nothing beats staying in a place where you feel most comfortable and relaxed. The Waialua Bay View Condominiums in Kapaa offers the same kind of relaxation with its beautiful oceanfront apartments. Range of activities includes snorkeling, swimming, diving, beach combing, hiking, meditation, sightseeing, shopping, golf, and dining in fancy restaurants. The Waialua Bay View Condominiums offers a very affordable studio type bedroom with a fully-equipped kitchen and a bathroom, perfect for the budget-conscious travelers. You may wish to have a barbecue party along the poolside and then head straight to the beach after a while. You may also take a short drive going to the island's north and south shores to get some fresh air and take photographs of the breathtaking views.

Kauai Sands Hotel

The Kauai Sands Hotel in Kailua is yet another relaxing haven for visitors of Kauai. You will even doze off just listening to the waves of this white sand beach spattering against the shores. Explore the oceanfront by jogging or strolling along the oceanfront.

Kauai Sands Hotel, known to be a Polynesian hotel, is very near the Coconut Market Place, where you can enjoy live entertainment. You can also shop around in about 60 boutiques within the area. Among the common island activities are boat tours with scuba diving, parasailing, deep sea fishing, and snorkeling. They are also helicopter tours, so visitors may take a peek at the majestic valleys and amazing waterfalls of Kauai's Grand Canyon.

Hideaway Bay Resort

This wonderful resort hotel is in a secluded location, but it still brings its visitors close to fine dining restaurants and many natural wonders of Kauai's North Shore. It provides luxury, comfort, and relaxation with its master bedrooms, complete with private baths, fully-equipped gourmet kitchens, king-size beds, and Jacuzzis. The resort is remarkably a vacation home very near to the Kilauea Lighthouse on the island of Kauai, which is the northernmost point of the main Hawaiian Islands built in 1913 to guide ships heading to and from the Orient.

The resort is tastefully designed in Hawaiian, Asian, and jungle motifs, allowing visitors to catch a glimpse of the breathtaking ocean views from every room. You will even get a chance to take peek at Mount Na-molo-kama while cooking in their fully equipped kitchen.

Your choices doesn't end here, of course. Aside from hotels and apartments, there also vacation homes and cottages to match the different taste and budget of tourists and travelers. If you're looking for ways to save on your travel spending, you'll be more than welcome to stay in bed and breakfasts and farmstays, which could make you feel more at home. But if you're looking forward to a luxurious vacation, then resorts and rental homes are among your best choices here in North Kauai.

Travelers are well advised to stay close to sites they wish to explore while in the North Shore. This will help them save time and even let them enjoy more activities during their stay. Every guest should at least have a map of North Kauai to know which places to visit and where to find a good place to stay

Fixed Budget

Found on the northernmost part of the Hawaiian chain, Kauai is one of the oldest islands. Although thousands of tourists come here every year, the "Garden Isle" has remained to be a haven for people who are in for a quiet escape. If you're looking for a getaway with minimum presence of tall hotels, dazzling city neon lights, and that migraine-inducing traffic, North Kauai would be an ideal choice for your vacation.

In these financially-draining times, a lot of individuals and families are having second thoughts about spending for a vacation, even if it is long overdue and much-deserved. If you are among them, it is possible to spend a holiday in North Kauai without using your life savings to the last cent. Here are some tips for a worthwhile North Kauai vacation even on a shoestring budget:

Save Up right from the get-go.
Before you even set foot on North Kauai, you should be able to make smart decisions with your travel spending. For your airfare, an

intelligent suggestion would be to scour for different rates from various airlines. One factor that will affect flight reservations would be the season, whether it's the holiday season or not in Hawaii. It is not a sure thing, but you may find it more affordable to go to North Kauai on a weekday, as opposed to a Saturday or Sunday. Most travel sites online would take care reservations for you, from hotel accommodation to car rental. It's all up to you to pick out the best deal.

Know where to stay.

The place where you will stay is a prime consideration for the cost of your accommodation and other travel expenses. You also have to take into account the duration of your vacation. Here in North Shore, Kauai, the ideal places to find a budget lodging is the stretch from Wailua to Kapaa.

Here are a few good suggestions:

Hale Hoo Maha - This is a tiny motel that offers spacious rooms at a good price. The establishment allows the following fun activities: horseback riding, surfing, golf, etc.

Kauai International Hostel - It has private rooms and dorms. This hostel is not a bad choice for your family; it has a game room, Internet access, and even bike rental facilities.

Tips for the budget conscious traveler

It cannot be denied, whether you are single traveler or with a family, that touring North Kauai could be very costly if you get careless in watching the expenses. What you can do instead is take note of the following tips to avoid spending too much on your vacation:

Tip #1: Assuming you are staying in a hotel, veer away from the breakfast buffet. A buffet could reach as high as around $30 per head, so how much would that sum up in a week for you and your spouse? If you do the math, you would realize that it is quite a hefty amount.

Thankfully, there are resorts with coffee shops. Going for fruits or pastries is not a bad idea at all. You could also ask the hotel manager if they offer an "ala carte breakfast special." Also, you do not need to eat in your hotel for every meal during the vacation. Befriend some locals, and they would be happy to direct you to the cheap-but-quality food restaurants.

Tip #2: Assuming you need to rent a car, get one that has enough space for you, your travel companions, and some travel bags. As much as possible, take your eyes off luxury cars or SUVs if you can find an economy car that also saves on gas. This would mean more savings that could be used in other things, say, shopping for souvenirs or going on a mountain climbing tour.

Tip #3: Don't let your tight budget limit the enjoyment of your vacation. Sure, there are things you can't do if you don't have enough cash, such as fine dining or staying in luxurious hotel rooms, but there are activities that can make up for this. For instance, instead of going to hotel restaurants, you can go to cafes for pastries or food stands for some local favorites such as the shave ice. You can also forget about tours and create your own itinerary. Being spontaneous can add to the excitement of your trip, so long as you won't get lost or spend mroe than you should.

Tip #4: Assuming you would be going on a tour, it would be better to book it way before your arrival. Many tour operators offer five to ten percent discounts if you book two weeks prior to the tour. Naturally, you cannot find a good discount tour if you won't take time to do some research. Online, you can search through tourism boards and for tour packages and do some comparison shopping of your own.

Low budget activities

Check out the Kokee State and Waimea Canyon Parks. Visit the lighthouse; this is a majestic view that would cost you nothing. While in Hawaii, also take time to watch the sunset. They say that the setting of the sun is more dramatic here than in any part of the world. The blue sky, cool breeze, and the verdant surroundings only make the scenery all the more breathtaking. Sunrise or sunset, you'll see couples and families gathered around the best viewing spots in North Kauai, where they also go on picnics. Another activity that is relaxing yet free is checking out the beautiful waterfalls. North Kauai has a number of them, and many of them are easy to access.

Naturally, a long vacation would not be complete if you and your family failed to visit the beaches. Anini Beach, Hanalei Bay, and Kee Beach are just among the many sites to choose from. A word of warning though: the North shore waters could have dangerous currents or waves, specially from October up to May. If you have young kids, it would be best to have them just watch the waves instead of wading in them.

North Kauai is a perfect spot for hiking, too. But unless you are a veteran hiker, it is not advisable to hike further than two miles. Usually, beyond this point, the trails could get a bit scary. Also, you might want to take your family to the Spouting Horn. It can be the most unforgettable blowhole in all of Hawaii.

Your choice of accommodation

For a budget vacation in North Kauai, staying in a condo also has its benefits. First, you get to save on accommodations. You could split, say, $200 per night with three of your friends, and that would mean some serious savings for all of you. Even if you are on your own, staying in a condo can also be budget-saving. For one, you could cook your own food. Usually, condo units come with fully furnished kitchen, complete with blenders, coffeemakers, toasters, grills, etc. Aside from these, you'll also enjoy the privacy of having the whole place only to you.

However, staying in a condo also has its downsides. One is that many of them do not have daily maid service. You would be making your own bed and have to get your own clean towels, among other things.

If you don't have money for staying in oceanfront hotels or luxurious hotels, there are cottages, farmstays, and vacation rentals to match your budget. Of course, you can also look for bed and breakfasts that could probably make you feel more at home as you mingle with the locals and other guests.

A final word

Even if you have a big sum at your disposal, it is not reason enough to throw money away without minding your options. Compared to other expensive cities around the world, here in North Kauai, you can still have a great time despite a limited budget. The Aloha spirit will make you feel more at home and comfortable even when staying in economy rooms. You can always look for "cheap eats" in this part of the island and sample the local favorites without having to wear fancy clothes or make reservations in fine dining restaurants.

For tours, you can always ask about the package deals. If they're too costly, perhaps you can have your own adventure with your a map as guide. You can always do your own research about places you are about to visit, so you can appreciate them more once you see them up close.

West Kauai

West Kauai is described as the intermingling of natural wonders and Hawaiian educational landmarks. There are many historical sites visit and cultural activities to explore here. That said, you may want to book your tours and complete vacation plans several weeks before the trip to the western side of Kauai. Here is a list of the places you should definitely explore while on vacation in this part of the island.

Waimea

Don't forget to jot down this place in your list of sites to explore in the western side of Kauai. Waimea is a very historical place, where the "Grand Canyon of the Pacific" is situated. The Canyon actually measures 10 miles long and 1 mile wide, while its depth is more than 3,500 feet. It was formed thousands of years ago by rivers and floods that flowed from Mount Waialeale's peak. The lines in the canyon walls indicate the various volcanic eruptions and lava flow it has experienced over the centuries.

This is a great place for sightseeing because of its astonishing panorama. The only problem is that along the 40-mile Waimea Canyon Road, it's difficult to find a gasoline station. Therefore, it's important for you to fill up your gas tank before embarking on this trip. If it's your first time to go to the Waimea Canyon, take Highway 50 west from Hanapepe toward Waimea, and you'll find it just right just past Mile Marker #23.

The sight of the ocean and the road along the canyon's western wall presents a view of shimmering streams and sugar canes planted on the hillsides. It's best to come during the morning and feast on the lunch wagon served at the Waimea Canyon Lookout.

The Grand Canyon shares with its admirers a magnificent panorama of its own island personality. The Canyon just can't help but exude its splendor. A diverse flora abounds in it including the yellow ginger, some eucalyptus trees, Kauai's own mokihana berries, and other plant species scattered on the 3,500-ft. elevation. The Waimea Canyon is a sight to behold that no one should dare miss.

The Captain Cook Monument

You can also find in Waimea the Captain Cook Monument, where British Captain James Cook first landed sometime in 1778. The Hawaiians treated Cook like a god, showering him with gifts and bestowing spiritual ceremonies in his honor. And when he returned, Captain James Cook toured the natives on his ships, accompanied by entertaining violin and flute concert, which fascinated the Hawaiian locals so much.

From this site, make it a point to also visit the Kealakekua Bay, which is a traditionally sacred site for the ancient Hawaiians. It will surely be much of a historical and cultural trip.

Polihale State Park

Before you get to the Polihale State Park, you definitely have to earn it. To set foot on this park is like having undergone a strenuous activity because of the rocky and unpaved road you have to go through before you will reach Polihale State Park. But this is no reason to be discouraged. The breathtaking sites will surely compensate for all your efforts. Instead of rushing to the site, why not go about it on a leisurely pace? This will surely take out some stress.

Once you've reached your destination, you will certainly enjoy gazing at one of the longest stretch of golden beaches where tourists sunbathing under the glare of the sun are found. Bounded by etched cliffs, blue sky, and spattering waves, it is no waste of time just staying there, getting mesmerized with the splendor of nature.

Kokee State Park

One of the most stunning and famous views in West Kauai is the Kalalau Valley, which is located at the end of the road in Kokee State Park. It is known to reveal a breathtaking waterfall, green pleated cliffs, and deep carved valley. The canyon is protected by the Koke'e State Park, which covers 4,345 acres of land and has 45 miles of trails that run through the canyon.

It is usually foggy in this area that is why hikers should choose to begin hiking with a trip to both Kalalau Lookout and the Puu okila Lookout. All park trails can sometimes be so muddy and slippery after heavy rains, which are quite common during winter months. So before you go hiking, always check first with the Natural History Museum for current advice on hiking trails. Also, get from the museum your personal maps of hiking trails, guided hikes, and forest workshops. Also, you may want to talk to the coordinator before you set foot on hiking. Go to the Ranger's Station, located at the Kokee Museum.

The best time to view the Kalalau valley is very early in the morning.

Hanapepe

Located along the banks of the Koula River, squeezed by Eleele and Kaumakani, Hanapepe was once in its lifetime considered Kauai's largest community. It is a historical place in West Kauai, with its century-old buildings looking so real, making the town of Hanapepe a favorite choice of film producers and directors.

Motion pictures such as "The Thornbirds" and "Flight of the Intruder" were set in this town that are known for its fine art works and galleries. Less than 10 art galleries of Hanapepe are listed among the gift shops and restaurants within the area. It is actually in the Hanapepe Valley Lookout that Steven Spielberg's "Jurassic Park" was filmed.

Come and discover Hanapepe Town's country charm. A trip to this town would mean historical education on your end, matched well with the actual Hanapepe Valley experience that reveals the magnificent beauty of a Hawaiian Valley. Aside from the manmade Hanapepe swinging foot bridge, you'll surely marvel at its thriving colors with a splash of green from its verdant surroundings, blue sky from above, and glimmering effect of the sun rays.

Salt Pond Beach Park

Visitors who have traveled to this part of Kauai describe Hanapepe as a glimpse of days gone by, particularly with the ancient Hawaiian salt pond near Hanapepe. The Salt Pond Beach Park is not just a crescent beach of white sands that is partially protected by a reef, but also a meeting place for swimming lovers in the west side of Kauai.

Worry no more about your kids swimming because it is a very safe in this beach the whole year round. Because of that, you do not need to be worried about your schedules, too. Camping is also allowed here, but only if you will present a County Permit, saying that you are allowed to do camping in the site.

Truly, the Salt Pond Beach is an awesome sight to behold. The waters look so inviting and relaxing. Its white sand spread on the ground, with the sun shimmering on it, making it look so golden and so beautiful to gaze at. Not only that, white sand beaches are also perfect for swimming and sunbathing.

The locals would share that their ancestors, and all Hawaiian families for that matter, have evaporated seawater in pans (which are dug out of red soil). This is how they produce natural sea salt during summer time. Then they bag the salt and use them for cooking and medicinal purposes. This practice has been observed from one generation to another. So when you chance upon visiting the park and see some saltmakers working the ponds, do not be surprised, you already know why.

Still not convinced? Don't take anybody's word for it. Go see for yourself what West Kauai has to offer for impassioned travelers like you.

How to Get to West Kauai

Getting to West Kauai is not that difficult, as you have several travel options to choose from. Almost all tourists will be coming from the Lihue Airport, the laid-back island's major airport which is a small terminal served with inter-island flights by several airlines. As Kauai's major airport, many car rental and shuttle services are available here.

Getting to West Kauai

From the airport, you can ride a taxi, opt for a shuttle service, or a bus ride. For more convenience, you can look for car rental services so that you can roam around West Kauai with more privacy. It's best to actually have car rental services booked in advance way before you land at the Lihue airport. This way, you won't have to worry about your transportation when you reach your destination.

Getting to West Kauai by bus

The west side of Kauai may also be reached by taking the Kauai Bus which offers limited service and schedules from Monday to Saturday, with numerous routes serving most areas of the island of Kauai.

Getting to West Kauai by car

If you decide to travel by car, you may take the highways 50 and 56, which are about two-thirds of Kauai's coastline. Highways 550 and 560 provide limited access to the interior island area.

This beautiful island of Kauai is comprised of two major highways, and the starting point of each begins in the busiest part of this tropical paradise, the town of Lihue where the hustle-bustle of Kauai goes on. And since you are planning to spend your vacation tour in the western side of the island, you must take the first route, which is the State Route 50, also known as the Kaumualii Highway. This path, which heads to the west, will pass through the various towns of Kalaheo, Hanapepe, Waimea, and Kekaha before finally reaching the end at the Na Pali Coast. The other route, on the other hand, is for heading north, so don't take that way. If you notice you are or your driver is heading to State Route 56, or taking the Kuhio Highway, and you are passing through the charming towns of Kapaa, Kilauea, Princeville, and Hanalei, ending at the other side of Na Pali, then that means you have taken the opposite way and need to retrace your path.

Upon reaching the west side of Kauai, you will instantly notice that this part has drier weather than the other areas of the island. It features hot, sunny beaches that stretch from Hanapepe to Waimea, Kekaha, and beyond. It will take you only about forty-five minutes to drive up from the coastline, going to the forested heights of Kokee State Park, which will definitely amaze you and your loved ones as it offers an entirely different world to its visitors.

For easier access to vacation destinations, you may avail of car rental services to provide you convenience and flexibility to explore the island. Buckling up in vehicles is very much a requirement every time aboard a vehicle, while all infants must be strapped properly into car seats or child seats. As in any place, pedestrians always have the right of way, but in Kauai, they also have the right of way even if they're not walking along the crosswalk. Just remember to always follow the "aloha" traffic rules while getting around in Kauai, which is to drive carefully, let your neighbors pass, and never to tailgate. Driving here is more laidback as this region is known for its laidback lifestyle.

Getting around in a bike

If you are thinking of how you can get around the island and explore while getting a lot of exercise, try biking. Bicycles, as well as bicycle maps, are available at biking facilities scattered throughout the area.

What to Do in West Kauai

Are you planning of going to Kauai for an active vacation? Go to the west side of Kauai and you will surely be welcomed to a paradise. The Garden Island of Kauai continues to prove its extraordinary blend of natural beauty and cultural heritage. Everyone visiting Kauai will surely enjoy the various fun and thrilling activities and adventures that the island offers. Whatever type of activity you're looking for, this region of Kauai is definitely the perfect place to visit.

First, you may start your exploration of the island by air, land, or sea, or by joining a group tour. Regardless of what your choice of tour is, you'll be able to witness in any angle, the beauty and grandeur of this garden paradise.

Activities you can participate in when visiting West Kauai include driving ATVs, surfing, biking, boogie boarding, hiking, trailing, horseback riding, and mountain tubing. See the island's amazing sights from exceptional vantage points you can access through air tours, windsurfing and kite surfing, water skiing, land tours, and ocean tours. Make sure you include the following activities in your itinerary:

Sailing

Kauai is beautiful in the morning and in the afternoons. But it is most beautiful during the sunset. No one will dispute that Kauai at its sunset turns into a more spectacular tropical getaway. To top this off, you and your loved one can have a romantic dinner and have an even more enchanted evening. There are so many boat companies that offer sunset cruising while a romantic dinner is served aboard their powered, sailing catamarans.

Sightseeing

With all the natural wonders West Kauai has to offer, sightseeing should definitely be included in your list of must-dos. Attractions you shouldn't miss include the amazing Waimea Canyon, a natural landmark that is a result of Hawaii's unique geography and landscape. There are several lookout points scattered around the canyon, giving you several options when gazing at this wonderful tourist attraction. Another sightseeing spot is the Kalalau lookout, a vantage point that boasts of incredible views and spectacular images of the Waimea Canyon.

The Hanapepe Valley lookout is also a must-see when in this part of Kauai. Because of its lush landscape, scenic greneries, and spectacular hills, this was actually used as a backdrop in the Hollywood movie Jurassic Park.

Strolling along the botanical gardens

If you don't mind traveling to nearby regions, then take a stroll along the botanical gardens of Kauai. You might be surprised to know that many native Hawaiian plant species are now endangered. There are three botanical gardens being operated on Kauai. And all these three share one common denominator: they are all devoted to addressing the conservation of the diversity of tropical plants, most especially the rare and endangered plant species, in the Hawaiian Islands. And you should come and see these botanical gardens since there are two on the South Shore and one on the North Shore, all open for public tours.

Bicycle tours

Biking is one activity that is for all ages and gives you physical exercise while you wander through the beaches, savoring going past through the hot and white beach sands stretching many miles long. Always remember to put on your safety gear such as helmets and elbow pads, and to familiarize yourself with what you can and cannot do when on a bike tour. If it's your first time to join a biking tour, stick to your guide and group. Going on a guided bike tour has several advantages. Aside from having someone to ask around when in an unfamiliar place, a guide can also narrate stories about Hawaiian history, culture, and folklore to make the trip more enriching. Enjoy your bike ride in this beautiful place and you'll learn about what makes Kauai special.

Eco-tours

The Kauai Eco-Tours are becoming popular with travelers nowadays. Visitors are now enjoying this outdoor activity involving travel to natural destinations and building environmental awareness. Many eco-tours also help provide financial assistance for conservation, and empowerment of local people and their culture. Satisfy your curiosity and ask your eco-tour guide about the different native Hawaiian plants, the various bird and trees species found in the island. You can also ask about the best hiking trails located in Koke'e State Park and Waimea Canyon State Park.

Snuba diving

If you don't know yet the difference between snorkeling and snuba, here it is: Snorkeling is such a great way to laze around in the sun, while floating cozily on the waters and marvel at schools of multi-colored fish coming up towards you. Snuba diving, on the other hand, is much more exciting because you get to move deeper into the bottom and therefore get a much clearer and more captivating view of the fishes swimming around.

Snuba, unlike scuba, which goes deep down the ocean bottom, is only a shallow water dive that is in the middle of snorkeling and scuba diving. Anyone can almost immediately learn to snuba in 90 minutes. But there are certain requirements that need to be satisfied such as that you must be at least eight years old, are healthy, and that you know how to swim. If you meet all these requirements, then you may start plunging into the water for your first snuba experience in Kauai.

Actually, snuba is not as exhausting and time consuming as learning to scuba, though snuba diving is a liitle bit more adventurous and satisfying than snorkeling. A float with a scuba tank serves as the air supply, giving you a chance to dive whenever you're ready. Experienced divers will serve as guide during your snuba diving tour, and they can help you identify the various marine life forms you'll see beneath the waters.

Shopping

If you love old, charming towns, West Kauai is the place to be. Located in this charming region is the Eleele Shopping Center, a place where you'll enjoy shopping for local handicrafts, scrumptious delicacies, souvenir items, and other knick knacks you can take home to remind you of your wonderful vacation. Other specialty products you'll find here include handmade soaps, furniture made of wood, and household items such as plates, cups, and pillows with Hawaiian motifs.

Eating out

After a day of adventure, satisfy your cravings and through the regions various eating establishments that include cozy eateries. Grab a lilikoi cream pie from a local bakery and savor the tropical flavor that makes Kauai unique. Whether you're looking for Thai, American, or Chinese dishes, Kauai's west side boasts of plenty of eating establishments that serve various cuisines. For a more unforgettable experience when in West Kauai, buy some grilled fish or Kalbi ribs and bring them with you when on a biking tour. At noon, feast on your delicious packed lunch while enjoying the majestic views.

Travelers who have been to Kauai come back and frequent the islands. Planning your paradise vacation in Kauai isn't difficult after all. Just always remember that it is not enough that you enjoy the natural and majestic beauty of Kauai; don't forget that when you plan your trip, you also make sure you book activities that will make the vacation one of the most memorable experiences of your life.

Kauai offers so much for explorers like you. You'll find a long list of fun and exciting activities, ranging from slightly active to madly exploratory. Whether you decide to tour with a group or go solo, the island's enchanting appeal is truly rewarding. Discover West Kauai, and make the most of your stay with the countless thrilling adventures you can choose from.

Where to Stay in West Kauai

Now that West Kauai has turned into another tourist hub, you can expect to find numerous accommodations in this part of the island. Aside from welcoming guests with the Aloha spirit, they offer temporary abode to visitors to make their stay all the more enjoyable. But with plenty of choices on where to stay in West Kauai comes the confusion and difficulty of having to narrow down the list of options.

Aside from thinking about a suitable type of accommodation for your budget and personal preference, knowing where to stay in this part of the island is also part of the whole consideration. Popular choices would be Waimea and Kekaha. You can find five-star resort hotels here with amenities such as gourmet breakfast, luxurious robes, private lanai, shuttle service, wireless Internet, fully equipped kitchen, Jacuzzi, and more. The list doesn't end here. Budget accommodations are also available for backpackers and those who are considering ways to save on vacation expenses.

The west side

The sunny west side of the island is home to several small towns, including the towns of Kekaha and Waimea. While in West Kauai, you can head straight to Kekaha Beach Park where you will surely enjoy the magnificent views of the Niihau Island. Spend some time to browse the art galleries of Hanapepe, Kauai's "Biggest Little Town," where so many Hawaiian works of art are exhibited.

Unwind and capture the never-ending views of the aquamarine Pacific Ocean, with the coconut palm trees swaying with the winds. The white and black sand beaches also draw in more visitors to this part of the island. Make sure that when you plan your vacation on the west side of Kauai, you will not miss the 10-mile long and 3,567-ft. deep Waimea Canyon, which is truly an astonishing sight for such an island this small in size. Drive up to the awesome Waimea Canyon, the "Grand Canyon of the Pacific," and see why you shouldn't miss this opportunity.

West Kauai accommodations

If looking for a place tp stay, here are some suggestions:

Kokee Lodge

Do not worry if you don't want to spend too much on this trip. West Kauai has various accommodations to match any budget, from luxurious to affordable rooms. It offers more budget-friendly bed and breakfasts as well as vacation rentals or homes with varying prices, comfort, and sizes. It's good to know that in the "Garden Isle," you won't run out of options just as easily.

If you plan to spend your vacation in West Kauai, Kokee Lodge is one good choice for you. Kokee Lodge offers cabins and dormitories, or units with separate bedrooms. Beddings, pillows, and linens will be provided, as well as kitchen utensils, should you need them for outdoor or indoor cooking. It has a cocktail lounge where you can stay for entertainment while drinking cocktails. There are also restaurants and gift shops.

Staying in Kokee Lodge is a good idea, specially if you have plans of hiking the Waimea Canyon and Kokee State Park. Waimea Canyon is the Pacific's largest canyon, as it measures 10 miles long and one mile wide. Not only that, it is more than 3,500-feet deep. Visitors who do not have much time anymore to go hiking or may be too tired to do this strenuous activity may still enjoy the roadsides in Kokee State Park.

Aston Waimea Plantation Cottages

Aston Waimea Plantation Cottages offers soothing spa treatments and many leisure activities for guests. This is situated in the middle of a 27-acre coconut grove, which is considered as private seaside cottages. Each room is creatively designed to reminisce or commemorate the way Hawaii used to be. The so-called historic rooms have been fully restored with modern amenities and conveniences. All bedrooms include a fully equipped kitchen. You are left to choose which among the one-, two-, three-bedroom units you want.

Plantation cottages and vacation homes

If you are the adventurous type who want to stay in other places aside from the mountains, then you might as well try the Waimea plantation cottages. They are sugar plantation cottages in the west side of Kauai. The cottages are appealing and inviting. Staying in any of them may seem like seeking refuge in a secluded haven with an oceanfront pool and tennis courts.

On the west side of Kauai, there are several Waimea cottages and Kekaha vacation rentals for accommodations and lodging, where the scenic views are just as exquisite but the prices are cheaper. If you want to make your life easier when deciding on your accommodation arrangements, simply go to Waimea and Kekaha areas, and you'll surely be given a wide range of cottages to choose from, from bungalows to luxury homes. Visitors may choose from family-friendly homes to luxury oceanfront vacation homes and beachfront villas in Pakala, Kekaha and Waimea in Kauai. All these locations are very ideal spots for kids because the surrounding area is covered in sugar cane fields. They are also not too far from Polihale Beach and Hanapepe. Come to the west side and see the longest white sand beach of 28 miles.

Kekaha bed and breakfast

Going on a vacation need not be very costly. A vacation will always be memorable for as long as you squeeze in various activities for the tour. West Kauai offers you a great number of places where you can stay without having to pay too much, while getting the best vacation ever. Imagine the marvelous sight of a 28-mile long white sand beach. As soon as you set foot on this beautiful island, explore the white sand beaches, which are just yards away from what could be your luxury vacation home. You may also go on hiking up the emerald colored-mountains of Kokee, or perhaps go on an adventurous boat tour to catch a glimpse of the breathtaking Na Pali Coast. After all these strenuous but enjoyable adventures, drop by the nearby restaurants for fine dining and be greeted with the Hawaiian natives' trademark of the Aloha spirit.

Kekaha vacation rentals
Go to the sunny west side of the island of Kauai and you'll see Kekaha Oceanside, a long stretch of white sand reaching up to 17 miles long. Kekaha is a very peaceful, rural community, which reflects the lifestyle of the Hawaiian natives during their plantation days. Most of Kekaha's vacation rental homes are actually historic plantation cottages that have just been remodeled and modernized, making them look like luxury beach homes and beautiful beach cottages.

More choices

If you prefer to stay in a secluded area with easy access to amenities and establishments, then West Kauai is a good choice. Perhaps an oceanfront resort or hotel will suit you best. Garden or mountain views are what you can expect from them. Some amenities also include spa treatments, golf courses, and a calming emerald tropical surroundings, with, of course, the best cuisines to offer.

The west side of Kauai is known to be secluded, calm, and serene, depicting the slow pace or laidback lifestyle of early settlers. There are never traffic jams, no crowded hotels or shops, or crowded restaurants and beaches to spoil your relaxation. Staying at a very peaceful place doesn't necessarily mean there is lack of activities. As a matter of fact, West Kauai has the best access to Kokee and Waimea Canyon National Parks, the Na Pali Coast, and one of the longest white sand beach in Hawaii for world-class surfing, diving, fishing, and sunset viewing.

Fixed Budget

If you are really eager to go visit the island of Kauai, but fear that you can't afford it, don't worry. You don't have to spend much on your vacation just to have the time of your life. The first step to make your shoestring budget work for you is to get familiar with the west side of

Hawaii. At least have a good idea of the sights to explore and things to do while staying in this part of the Hawaiian island. A little research will save you a great deal of stress, not to mention, earn you some savings. With that, you can focus on things your budget will let you enjoy.

For places to stay, know that there are vacation home rentals and resort hotel accommodations in the island to match any kind of traveling budget. After choosing the right accommodation for you, the one that won't really hurt your pocket, you must plan well for your cheap adventures. You may avoid the more costly activities such as the helicopter or plane tours and settle for sightseeing, hiking, or camping, and many other worthwhile and exciting adventures that won't require you to pay too much. Don't think that all vacations should be expensive for you to have fun. Not in West Kauai.

Budget accommodations

When planning to stay in the west side of Kauai, you will fancy getting the budget-friendly offers from various resort hotels and lodges such as the Kokee Lodge. There are also countless vacation rentals or home rentals with varying sizes and prices, each giving you different degrees of comfort.

Kokee Lodge offers cabins and dormitories, or units with separate bedrooms. Beddings, pillows, and linens are provided, along with kitchen utensils for outdoor or indoor cooking. It also has a cocktail lounge where you can stay for entertainment, a restaurant, and a gift shop.

Waimea's plantation cottages also let you indulge in the soothing spa treatments and leisure activities. The Aston Waimea Plantation Cottages are in the middle of a 27-acre coconut grove. Each room is creatively designed to show how Hawaii used to be. The so-called historic rooms have been fully restored with modern amenities and conveniences. One-, two-, and three-bedroom units are available with fully equipped kitchen.

Also, you must consider looking at the Waimea cottages and Kekaha vacation rentals for accommodations and lodging. The scenic vistas they offer are amazing, specially when seen right from your room window. The good news is that they don't cost as much as staying in a luxurious hotel. Visitors may choose from budget and family-friendly homes in Pakala, Kekaha and Waimea in Kauai. These locations are also ideal for kids, who can run freely in sugar cane fields or play relentlessly in white sand beach.

You can also schedule your trip during the off-peak season. Aside from getting cheaper deals for travel and accommodations, you may also enjoy getting around West Kauai without throngs of tourists. This is best for people who are in West Kauai to escape the hustle bustle of city life and would like to seek refuge in the island's laidback atmosphere.

Cheap food

Aside from accommodations and tours, another big concern is the food. Travelers, specially those from another country, would love to sample local Hawaiian cuisine. After a tiring activity, most would surely welcome a feast of homegrown dishes or desserts to keep them full.

It's good to hear that in West Kauai, good food doesn't come at a price you can't afford. If you're traveling with your family or friends, then Lappert's Hawaii in Hanapepe deserves a visit. It is known as a kid-friendly place that serves different flavors of ice cream, baked goodies, and even coffee. It is a popular choice for sweet treats. They offer fresh servings in small batches. This means that you don't have to burn a hole in your pocket just to indulge in your sweet cravings while enjoying the Aloha spirit that surrounds the place.

If you're looking for fresh fruits and market produce, you should drop by the farmer's market. Fruits and vegetables here are not only inexpensive but also fresh. When driving along the Poipu area, you'll find a fruit stand on the side of the road. If you're a bit unsure what to add to your fruit basket, you can take a bite of the fruit before buying it.

To scrimp on your travel spending, you may also want to go to grocery stores and find some basic essentials for picnic lunches. You may also prepare meals on your lanais and balconies to help save money while having a great time doing so.

Of course, your choice for "cheap eats" aren't limited with these suggestions. Just by driving around, you can find food stands and restaurants that offer great menu choices, even if they're not exactly gourmet dishes. You can also get yourself a map with a list of dining establishments to help you find a good place to eat with your budget. Just remember that good food doesn't have to be served only with silver spoon or expensive china. Be open to sampling true Island Rim flavors even from food stands.

Cheap activities

You don't need to spend much when touring West Kauai. You may decide to just go hiking up the Waimea Canyon, the largest canyon in the Pacific (measuring about 10 miles long, 1 mile wide and more than 3,500-feet deep). Or, if you do not want to get too tired, then you might as well take a stroll at the Kokee State Park. Sightseeing and cycling are among the least expensive activities you can enjoy while staying in the west side of Kauai.

Of course, being budget conscious doesn't mean that you can no longer have fun on your vacation. You just have to put your best efforts on finding dining places where you can enjoy good food for less. Instead of booking yourself an expensive tour, you can have your own adventure and let your feet take you to interesting sights, as you roam around the island. A little spontaneity won't hurt your vacation.

It will also be wise to shop for souvenir items at thrift shops. Look for things that can only be found in Kauai or will best describe what the place is like for your family or friends back home. While in the west side of Kauai, take time to do some nature walks. Enjoy the laidback setting and serene atmosphere of this part of the island. If you're an artist, musician, or writer, draw inspiration from the scenic views of the rolling valleys and endlessly flowing waterfalls.

Instead of renting a car, why not try mountain biking? Bicycle maps are available in the tourist center. You may also want to check for cultural shows in the island that run for free, as well as check the schedules for whale watching. There are usually luaus or free hula shows in the area.

Truth of the matter is, you don't need huge bucks with you to have fun; the beauty and magnificence of nature is enough to make you feel excited and occupied. All you will really need is a simple accommodation that will provide you comfort and convenience, a rental car or bike to give you flexibility to roam around, and the enthusiasm to discover what West Kauai has to offer.

It might do you good to explore beyond the commercialized areas of the island. This way, you'll get more meaning and value from your vacation.

www.ingramcontent.com/pod-product-compliance
Lightning Source LLC
Chambersburg PA
CBHW021101080526
44587CB00010B/328